Why?

EXPLORING FAITH

Donald MacEwan

University Chaplain, University of St Andrews

Something has led you to read this book. I don't know what it is, perhaps you're not completely sure either, but something has drawn you to explore. For now, you may not even be sure what you're exploring. That's fine. After all, if you knew what you were exploring, it wouldn't be exploring – it would be more like recognising what you've already sorted out. There are lots of different books for that: this is about exploring.

What could be out there, in this journey, which you haven't mapped before? It could be God, or Jesus, or spirituality. Or a desire to live a better life, to have healthier relationships. Or it could be about making connections with other people who have faith, or finding a home for your faith, or being part of a church. Or it could be about working out if you have faith, and what your faith is in, and what faith feels like. It could be about how that faith changes you.

Somehow you have decided to explore the Christian faith. And that's what we'll do in the sections which follow. But just before we do, isn't there a major problem? Surely we can't just plunge in to what the Bible says, and what Christians believe. Exploring is about questioning, and we will consider some of the following:

- What about suffering? How can we think that God exists?
- Does Christian faith really stand up to secularist claims?
- Has science not discredited religious claims?
- What about my own personal doubts?
- Why are there so many different Churches?

These are serious questions, and exploring the Christian faith has to mean exploring some of these problems. So in between the sections on the Christian faith we'll also look at these questions. You're welcome to read those sections first, or just look at them when they come – they are marked with a green border so they are easy to find.

Faith and doubt

One difficult question is worth looking at first. What about faith? How does faith come about? Here's an example from my life. Recently I went to a jazz concert. I could tell the tunes were good and the musicians were brilliant but I just didn't get it. Everyone else was loving it, and I wanted to love it, but instead I sat stonily unmoved. How would an appreciation of jazz come to me? How does faith come to anyone?

First of all, what is faith – in particular, the faith a Christian has? I think it has two parts. One is a number of beliefs – for example that God exists, that Jesus is the Son of God, that the Holy Spirit is with us, and other objects of belief, which we'll explore especially when looking at the Creed.

The other is that faith is also about belief *in* God, trust *in* God, and faith *from* God. This is belief *in* God who won't let us down, God who is there for the world, faith we can never fall deeper than God's loving arms. Faith then is a relationship. Whenever this book talks about faith, it may help you to think of it as trust, as the form of a relationship. But even as a relationship of trust, faith can be slippery.

Faith is a relationship.

Here's a story from the Bible which may help. Jesus meets a man whose son is seriously unwell. The man says:

> 'if you are able to do anything, have pity on us and help us.' Jesus said to him, 'If you are able! – All things can be done for the one who believes.' Immediately the father of the child cried out, 'I believe; help my unbelief!' (Mark 9:22b–24)

In this person, belief and unbelief, faith and doubt live side by side. I think that's true for most people, and for most Christians. Faith is not just knowledge, and so there is very often a sense that things may not be quite as we believe. Or indeed, that our faith is completely wrong. I am not the only Christian who sometimes has the sudden thought, *What if it's all a complete mistake?* It's okay to acknowledge we have doubts. The world won't cave in and the church roof won't fall. Sometimes it's in exploring our doubts that our faith becomes deeper.

It's also the case that faith does not always come when we want it. There are people who long to believe, who pray and pray, and who would dearly love to find God is real to them – but scepticism proves stronger (like me and jazz). On the other hand there are also people who find that no matter what happens to them, including deep personal tragedies, their faith stubbornly refuses to melt away, that they cannot *not* believe in God.

But for many and perhaps most people, there is a sense that faith can grow, or deepen, if we encourage the presence of God in our lives. This can happen as we explore the faith. Here are some ways in which we can allow faith to deepen:

- Reading this publication or other material.
- The Bible – try reading the verses outlined in the 'Read' sections.
- Try praying – such as saying the Lord's Prayer on page 73.
- Worship – attend your local church; the Church of Scotland website has a Church Finder app to help you find your local congregation.
- Imagination – imagine situations assuming the loving presence of God.

It is different for different people. But faith is not static, and it's exciting to feel it growing.

Something has led you here. And whatever it is, I hope you feel free to explore your faith and your doubt. ∎

READ

Psalm 34:1–10 Taste and see that the Lord is good

Mark 9:14–27 The father of an ill son believes

Acts 16:16–34 A jailer becomes a believer in God

Dave Tomlinson, **How to be a Bad Christian... And a Better Human Being**, (London: Hodder & Stroughton, 2012) Section 1

Gilleasbuig Macmillan, **A Workable Belief: Thoughts on the Apostles' Creed**, (Edinburgh: Saint Andrew Press, 1993) Section 2

Rowan Williams, **Tokens of Trust: An Introduction to Christian Belief**, (London: Canterbury Press, 2007) Section 1

THINK

1. What has led you to read this book?

2. Is there an objection to faith which looms large in your mind?

3. Do you have faith *and* doubt? When does faith tend to be stronger? And when does doubt tend to be stronger?

ACT

Take five minutes to note your initial thoughts and the questions you have right now about Christian faith. What one question stands out for you?

WHAT IS A CHRISTIAN?

Donald MacEwan
University Chaplain, University of St Andrews

What is a Christian? In some ways this is a deceptively simple question. It looks as if all we have to do is find the marks that distinguish a Christian and we have the answer. After all, if we ask, 'What is a fridge magnet?' it's pretty straightforward to answer – it's a magnet which you put on a fridge. But with a Christian it's as if there's a number of overlapping aspects which contribute to the answer – and there can be grey areas. Here are some possible answers:

A Christian is someone who lives in a Christian country. This cannot be the whole truth. For one thing, our country is much more varied than before, with people of different religions and philosophies of life. At the same time, our heritage has been influenced by the Christian tradition including laws, education and family patterns. So while living in a particular country does not make an individual a Christian, it may form the background for our explanation of faith.

A Christian is someone from a Christian family. This too cannot be the whole truth. Christians can have atheist parents, and Christian parents can have atheists for children. But we are influenced, in faith as much as in any aspect of life, by our upbringing. People who approach the Church to be married, for example, often say that they were brought up in the Church and so it feels the right place for their wedding, even if they do not currently go to church very often. So while being part of a family does not make an individual a Christian, it may form the immediate context for our basic understanding of God and Jesus.

A Christian is someone who lives a Christian life. This is true, but again is not everything that we mean by *Christian*. Christians should aspire to be loving and kind, honest and generous, concerned for the weak and the vulnerable – even if they sometimes fall short. Christians are not unique in having such virtues. There is a large overlap in good human action between Christians and people more generally, people of different faiths and philosophies of life. Some of Jesus' moral teaching has echoes in other wisdom. So there is more to being a Christian than living a Christian life (though it matters).

Our country, family background and our way of life may all contribute to our understanding of being a Christian. But another ingredient is required: trust. Specifically, trust in Jesus Christ.

Trust

Faith is more than belief that statements about God and Jesus are true: it is a trust in God. Christian faith then is trust in Jesus with our lives. This means believing that Jesus, who lived, died and was raised to life, is God. It means trusting in Jesus as the one who will rescue us from the wrong place, help us in all things, and guide us in the way of generous love. We entrust our lives to Jesus: we say we cannot, on our own, rescue ourselves, help ourselves or guide ourselves – we need Jesus. With this, all the aspects of our lives change – and the result is a Christian.

66 there can be grey areas.

A Christian is a work in progress. Some days we trust a little more, some days a little less. Our Christian lives can be distinctly wobbly, as we face challenges from relationships, work and the culture around us. Our belief in God can be upset by questions of suffering, or the actions of human beings including Christians. Christians are, by definition, not perfect – as we acknowledge our need for Jesus, we recognise our flaws and our failings. But Christians live in the trust that God is with them, shaping them, helping them become ever more Christian, ever more like Jesus.

When people think about joining the Church, they sometimes feel that their faith is not firm enough, that they have not been a Christian for long enough, that they get too much wrong. They think that a church member is the finished article. But anyone who spends any time in churches will know that church members, sometimes of many years' standing, also struggle with faith, and get things wrong. The best churches have room for doubt, and also the honesty to challenge people to live a more loving and generous life. It's not really about celebrating the triumph of coming to faith, more about looking forward to deepening in trust, growing in love, delighting in service.

Profession of Faith

Let's begin to look, then, at the Church of Scotland's service for Profession of Faith. Candidates for membership are asked this question:

Do you reject sin,
confess your need of God's forgiving grace,
and pledge yourself to glorify God
and to love your neighbour?

If you can answer yes, you are saying that you are a Christian. This is how the Church of Scotland understands being a Christian. Let's look at it line by line.
Do you reject sin? Being a Christian involves a turning – towards God, but also away from sin. What is sin? It's easy to think of examples – magazines focus on issues around the body, from sex scandals to overindulgence. And the news features wrongdoing which society rejects, from phone-hacking to fiddling expenses. But sin is much broader and deeper than individual actions. It refers to the general and inescapable tendency which humans have to live for ourselves, to be self-centred, to be limited in our love, to trust ourselves rather than God. Sin is not merely about wrongdoing in matters of sex or money, honesty or power. It is a force which affects every aspect of life, every thought or feeling, all speech and action.

Christians reject sin. This doesn't mean that Christians never make mistakes, behave badly or mess up relationships at home, at work, among friends or within the church. It does mean that as Christians we try not to live according to ourselves, for ourselves. We acknowledge the pull of sin, the temptation to live selfishly, the apparent attraction of fruits of a life without God. But we aim to turn away from that: to live for God, to trust in Jesus, and to live as followers of Jesus, loving generously. 'As God's chosen ones, holy and beloved, clothe yourselves with compassion, kindness, humility, meekness, and patience' (Colossians 3:12).

Confess your need of God's forgiving grace. Being a Christian means recognising our self-centredness, and how our speech, action and way of life can hurt ourselves and others. It means realising we can't get ourselves out of this tendency on our own: the more we try to extricate ourselves from selfishness, the more we entrust ourselves with the power to do so, and the more deeply we become self-centred. It's a bit like getting lost when driving in a strange place – the more we take another turn the further we get lost, and the more frustrated we become. We need someone outside us to rescue us, and show us where to go (or at least a trustworthy SatNav).

God's forgiving grace is the way we are saved from being lost. The love that God has for people is so deep and unconditional that it finds us when we are lost. God's love is not lessened when we hurt others or ourselves, but sets us right when we're on the wrong road. Forgiveness is often the hallmark of loving relationships – parents and children, brothers and sisters, husbands and wives, partners and friends. In a way, that forgiveness is a reflection of the basic, unceasing love of God which never gives up on creation, despite all the ways we go wrong. The story of Jesus Christ, his birth, life, death and resurrection is the story of God's forgiving love towards creation. *Grace* is the single word the New Testament often uses to summarise this unconditional, forgiving love of God found in Jesus Christ. 'God, who is rich in mercy, out of the great love with which he loved us even when we were dead through our trespasses, made us alive together with Christ – by grace you have been saved – and raised us up with him …' (Ephesians 2:4–6).

And pledge yourself to glorify God. In other words, forgiveness is not an end in itself. Christians respond to God's forgiving grace in faith and in love. Glorifying God is a way of saying we respond to God by acknowledging who God is and what God has done. We don't give ourselves the glory for the ways we reject sin, or for being forgiven, or for finding the right road for life. The point is that by ourselves we could not get there. Instead, we give God the glory – God is the one whose love has found us. We glorify God by acknowledging his presence in creation, and his profound influence in our lives. We do this in worship and prayer, by thanking God, and by acting and speaking in ways which acknowledge our dependence on his never-ceasing, graceful love.

And to love your neighbour. Being a Christian is about a transformed life – turning from self-centredness to a life that acknowledges the need to love God and to love those around us. This life requires a love from beyond ourselves. It's a life which responds in humble gratitude. And it's a life which follows Christ in his life, full of integrity, compassion and risk. The pledge to love our neighbour is a shorthand for this, a shorthand commended by Jesus himself, for example in Mark 12:28–31:

> One of the scribes … asked him [i.e. Jesus], 'Which commandment is the first of all?' Jesus answered, 'The first is, "Hear, O Israel: the Lord our God, the Lord is one; you shall love the Lord your God with all your heart, and with all your soul, and with all your mind, and with all your strength." The second is this, "You shall love your neighbour as yourself." '

Who is our neighbour? Jesus told a story about a good Samaritan which explores this. Our neighbour, he implies, is not merely someone close to us, from our in-group. It could be a stranger, even an enemy. Being a Christian is about the journey from simply loving ourselves to loving those in the world around us. ∎

READ

Luke 15:11–32 A story of two sons and a gracious father

Romans 3:21–26 All have sinned; grace as a gift

Ephesians 2:1–10 God who is rich in mercy

Brian Draper, **Searching 4 Faith**, (Oxford: Lion Hudson, 2006) Section 6

Francis Spufford, **Unapologetic: why, despite everything, Christianity can still make surprising emotional sense**, (London: Faber and Faber, 2012)

Nick Baines, **Finding Faith**, (Edinburgh: Saint Andrew Press, 2009)

THINK

1. How would you define a Christian?

2. What, if any, is your experience of grace?

3. In what way would you show love to a stranger or an enemy?

ACT

What one thing could you do to be more help to others?

My Story **Kay Slater**

When I think about my own journey of finding faith, I remember that for me it was a gradual awakening process where God's presence and love began to enter into my heart. I've heard many people question how one can have strong faith in God when there is no evidence that God exists. I have taken a long time to ponder that question and I believe with all my heart that God is within us all by his Spirit. The question is whether our souls are open to welcome God into our lives.

When I opened my heart to Jesus and put my trust in him, I almost felt as if I was blinded by such warm and bright sun rays that I could no longer see the world as I had before. Jesus is that light which can enter our lives so brightly that we need never worry about darkness. Jesus' light changes our perception of life and of how we ought to live and treat others. This change that I am describing is a change within us; it's within our hearts.

My journey of faith is ever growing, and for the past few years I have begun to see God's grace and love all around me. I can feel God when I'm surrounded by nature or when I look at the sunrise in the morning. I see Jesus' presence in the kindness of people's hearts or the joyful noise of genuine laughter between friends and family. For God is goodness, life, energy and above all, God is love!

For me, faith and religion are two separate entities, and personally I have never relished the word religion as I feel that throughout history it has been a cause for conflict and violence. Instead, I would say that I have a deep faith and love in Jesus and that each day I try my best to follow and listen to him. That is why I believe that faith is truly about finding a personal connection with Jesus. When I reflect upon my first experiences of reading the New Testament and searching for God through prayer, I feel it was around that time that I truly met Jesus, accepted him and promised to follow him every day for the rest of my life.

I believe that living our lives for others, showing love and trying to forgive is the best way to follow close to Christ. Each day I thank God for the goodness and love that I have been blessed with in my life. I believe that Jesus is always here with each and every person who searches for him. He went through such suffering for us, and we are forgiven for our wrongs. I have given my heart and soul to Jesus and my faith shows me that love is the greatest gift that I can give.

APOSTLES' CREED

The Church of Scotland believes in God, Father, Son and Holy Spirit, and proclaims Jesus Christ crucified, risen and glorified.

Our standards of belief are to be found first in the Old and New Testament (the Bible), and then in the Church's historic Confession of Faith. For a brief summary of Christian beliefs, it is useful to look at the Apostles' Creed, which is used by many Christian churches in declaring Christian faith:

I believe in God, the Father almighty,
creator of heaven and earth.

I believe in Jesus Christ,
God's only Son, our Lord,
who was conceived by the Holy Spirit,
born of the Virgin Mary,
suffered under Pontius Pilate,
was crucified, died, and was buried;
he descended to the dead.
On the third day he rose again;
he ascended into heaven,
he is seated
at the right hand of the Father,
and he will come to judge
the living and the dead.

I believe in the Holy Spirit,
the holy catholic Church,
the communion of the saints,
the forgiveness of sins,
the resurrection of the body,
and the life everlasting.

Amen

Who?

I BELIEVE IN GOD

Donald MacEwan
University Chaplain, University of St Andrews

God is not in a single place or time.

It is time to explore more deeply the content of Christian faith. The Church of Scotland often uses the Apostles' Creed because it sets out the essentials of the Christian faith. When people are baptised, or join the Church, they are asked to affirm their faith in the words of the Apostles' Creed. This is a creed (a summary of what Christians believe) going back to the first centuries of the Christian Church and has been used in baptism services in many places. The Apostles' Creed is separated into three sections, corresponding to God the Father, Son and Holy Spirit. We'll look at these sections in turn.

In the service of baptism and/or confirmation (in which people join the Church), the minister asks the candidates:

Do you believe in God
who made you and loves you?

This question leads to the answer, which is the whole first section of the Apostles' Creed:

I believe in God, the Father almighty,
creator of heaven and earth.

Do you believe ...? I believe ...
Belief in the Christian faith is at least a twofold phenomenon. It is belief that certain statements about God are true, but it is also belief in God, trust in God with whom we're in a relationship. All three sections in this translation of the Apostles' Creed begin: I believe in ... All three have this double sense: believing certain truths about God as Father, Son and Holy Spirit, and doing so trusting in God with our lives.

God
Christians believe in God. In some ways it's hard to tease out this brief sentence without immediately turning to the next words (*the Father almighty*) and indeed the rest of the Creed. But it's worth lingering for a while. Images of God are quite hard to come by. They tend to be bearded male figures, from the Sistine Chapel to Morgan Freeman in *Bruce Almighty*. But there is something in the concept of God which resists being pictured. God is unlike everything in creation. God has no shape, no size, no colour.

God has no beginning in time, no built-in obsolescence. God is not in a single place or time. God does not need oxygen or food or shelter. God is not changed by the passing of time. There's a whole approach to God which emphasises these negatives, in which people come to God by way of acknowledging what God is not.

There's also an approach which explores what God is like by way of thinking about what is good in creation, and seeing God as like that, only beyond what creation is capable of. Imagine the most gorgeous late evening light, picking out every rise and fall of coastal dunes – God is like that light, only infinitely more beautiful. Imagine the deepest human wisdom distilled over centuries of enquiry – God is like that wisdom, only infinitely wiser. Imagine the most courageous, generous, self-sacrificial person who pours out their life for others – God is like that person, only infinitely more loving.

Between these ways, acknowledging both what God is not, and what may give a dim picture of God, we may come to some understanding of what God is like. But turning to the next words, the content fills out, reflecting on God as encountered in the Bible.

The Father Almighty

Those images of God – male and bearded – also reflect this line in the Creed. Christians believe in God as Father. While the Bible offers a number of images of God, the Old Testament occasionally refers to God as Father – of the nation of Israel, or of individuals including orphans. But in the New Testament, God is much more often referred to as Father, and prayed to as Father. Jesus regularly called God his Father, most notably when he taught his disciples to pray, in what we call The Lord's Prayer (see page 73), which you may well have prayed many times in church.

This may be so familiar that it's easy to lose the significance. First, does this mean that God is male? While it's true that the Bible, and most Christian writings, predominantly use the pronouns *he*, *him* and *his* for God, the Christian faith does not emphasise the maleness of God, and also draws on female images in its depiction of God. Indeed, a more profound understanding is that God is beyond the distinctions of sex found in creation, or perhaps that God incorporates both male and female. Genesis 1:27 is intriguing:

> So God created humankind in his image,
> in the image of God he created them;
> male and female he created them.

When we refer to God as Father, it is not his maleness we refer to but something that belongs to fatherhood, or perhaps we should say parenthood. We trust in God who is loving and caring, as parents are called to be, who gives children life, speaks to them, teaching and guiding, who looks out for them when they explore their own freedom, showing them the right path and helping them see when and how they have gone wrong, who forgives them, who delights in them as they mature, who longs for their fulfilment.

Of course, there are people who find this aspect of the Christian faith troubling. Their own experience of their parents may not have been marked by love and care. They find it difficult to trust God as Father. It's helpful here to realise that God is not only Father, but that we trust in God who is beyond fatherhood or motherhood or parenthood; God is beyond the distinctions of sex and gender found in creation. Imagery is imagery, and while there is ample scriptural and church warrant to call God our Father, it is possible and perhaps helpful for some Christians to find other ways to think of God and to be able to trust God.

Almighty is an adjective which expresses Christians' trust in God's power. Christians believe that God is all-powerful, and there is evidence for this in the immense size and complexity of the universe as a whole and the variety of life as we know it. But this is not a power which God exercises randomly. Although God may have the power to do all things, he clearly does not do all things. *Father* qualifies *almighty* – and so we trust God to exercise power in a loving, caring way, guiding rather than controlling, granting freedom rather than coercing obedience. But *almighty* does express our conviction that God is not lesser or even equal in power to any other force, such as another god, or an evil power, or evil itself. There is nothing which could overwhelm God, no-one who can thwart God. No matter what happens in creation, from earthquakes to acts of terrorism, God is not defeated and his power of love continues to work, and to shine, in the darkest of places. Consider this further with the article on page 26 about suffering.

Creator of heaven and earth

Christians believe in God, creator of heaven and earth. The topic of creation has become something of a battle ground in recent debates. Some critics of Christianity say that it should be abandoned because science now explains heaven and earth. Earth – from its rocks to its seas, its land and its atmosphere, its sun and moon, its plants and animals, its human beings in body and mind – can, they say, be explained by maths, physics, chemistry and biology. Astronomers increasingly discover the history of the universe, and predict its future. There is no need for a Creator in a nature whose laws, processes and evolution are increasingly understood.

But Christians have rightly responded that while it is one thing to say that science has the power to understand what happened in the Big Bang, how the laws of nature interact, and how life has evolved on earth, it is quite another to say that there is no creator. When Christians say they believe in God, creator of heaven and earth, this does not mean that they are anti-science. In fact, the opposite is true. Christians are often filled with wonder and delight at the findings of scientists, in discovering how the universe has been shaped, how life has emerged, and the delicate interplay of eco-systems. Many scientists are themselves Christians – for more on *faith and science*, see page 42.

66 earth is created by God, who is love.

However, Christians do have a presupposition that not all scientists share. And that is that the world and everything in it depends on God for its being. Without God, there would be no stars and planets, pine-trees or beetles. *Creator* does not mean that Christians believe that God fashioned in some heavenly workshop every single sub-atomic particle, but rather that every single particle owes its existence to there being a Creator. God's will was to create and for there to be a creation, for there to be matter which is *not* God, in and through and to which God can offer love.

The Bible was written with what is to us a rudimentary understanding of nature and the natural world. But its conviction that the world depends on God is one which Christians continue to believe. Writing about living things on land and sea, the psalmist sings:

These all look to you
    to give them their food in due season;
when you give to them, they gather it up;
    when you open your hand, they are filled with good things.
When you hide your face, they are dismayed;
    when you take away their breath, they die
    and return to their dust.
When you send forth your spirit, they are created;
    and you renew the face of the ground. (Psalm 104:27–30)

Given that earth is created by God, who is love, we trust in God who loves this world. Although there is now significant scientific evidence that the account of evolution by natural selection is true (even if certain details are disputed), Christians infer from our conviction that God is Creator, that God delights in creation, its variety and fertility, its colour and shape, its sounds and scents, its beauty, and the emergence within it of animals capable of love, of tenderness, of speech and of joy, of art and of science. It follows that as part of our response to God, glorifying God and loving our neighbour, we respect and honour creation.

Sadly, much human interaction with creation in recent centuries has been exploitative, seeing no virtue in other species, their habitats, and the environmental conditions for complicated eco-systems. Climate change is the most obvious though not the only environmental issue which we urgently need to face. Christian belief in God, creator of heaven and earth, should lead us to be active in care for our planet, and all to whom it is home.

Contemporary debates have focussed on earth (encompassing all of the universe), but we say we believe in God, creator of heaven as well as of earth. This refers to the created realm invisible to us, and not explored by science, which is the abode of God and of the angels. Again, in the Lord's Prayer, Jesus teaches us to pray to 'Our Father, who art in heaven' or simply 'Our Father in heaven'. Heaven is the transcendent realm within creation from which God acts. ■

READ

Genesis 1–2 Stories of Creation

Psalm 139:1–18 Where can I go to escape you?

Acts 17:16–33 Paul proclaims God in Athens

Keith Ward, **The Big Questions in Science and Religion**, (Pennsylvania: Templeton Foundation Press, 2008)

Rowan Williams, **Tokens of Trust: an introduction to Christian belief**, (Norwich: Canterbury Press, 2007) Sections 1 & 2

Tom Wright, **Simply Christian**, (London: SPCK Publishing, 2011) Section 5

THINK

1. What picture, if any, comes to mind when you think about God?

2. What does it mean to you to say that God is almighty?

3. Can you be a scientist and believe in God as creator? Are there things that science has taught us which undermine Christian faith?

ACT

Go for a walk in nature, and consider what it might mean to believe that the universe was all created by God.

MORE ABOUT THE APOSTLES' CREED

Paul Nimmo

Professor in Systematic Theology, University of Aberdeen

T he Apostles' Creed is a text that goes back to the early centuries of the Christian faith and continues to be used in Churches such as the Church of Scotland today. The word 'creed' comes from the Latin 'credo', meaning 'I believe', and the Apostles' Creed sets out a short summary of the fundamental beliefs of the Church. The Apostles' Creed is used in many Churches, and appears in the Church of Scotland hymn-book (628 in CH4). However, it is but one of a series of important early creedal statements of the Church, with the similarly ancient Nicene Creed also appearing in the Church of Scotland hymn-book (649 in CH4).

Despite the name, it is not the case that the wording of the Apostles' Creed goes back to the apostles themselves. The actual history of the Apostles' Creed is rather complex and greatly disputed. In its current form and content, the text is not found until early in the eighth century, where it is cited in Latin in the work of a monk called Priminius. But earlier versions of broadly the same text had been circulating for a century or two before this time in the south-west of what is now France. Similar texts, also supplying a brief outline of the teaching of the Christian faith, had been used as creedal statements since the early centuries of the Church.

Such early creedal statements developed directly from the body of Christian teaching and preaching found in the writings of the New Testament. Hence it is no surprise that the beliefs expressed in the Apostles' Creed can also be traced back to scripture. Even if there is no direct literary connection between the Apostles' Creed and the apostles themselves, the name of the Creed remains significant: it indicates that the content of the Creed agrees with the teaching of the apostles, and therefore with the message of Jesus Christ. Calling the creed the Apostles' Creed indicates that its teaching is in the apostolic tradition, and thus authentically Christian.

The Apostles' Creed follows the pattern of many early creeds (and some scriptural texts) in having a three-fold pattern: moving from God the Father, through God the Son/Jesus Christ to God the Spirit. The pattern expresses the Christian belief that God is a Trinity, both Three and One. The material following the profession of belief in the Father and in the Son is largely a report of their activities – the Father is connected with the act of creation, while the Son is identified with the historical narrative of the events described in the Gospels: from conception; through incarnation, passion, crucifixion, burial, resurrection and ascension; to judgement.

the Apostles' Creed sets out a short summary of the fundamental beliefs of the Church.

READ

William Barclay, **The Apostles' Creed**, (Louisville: Westminster John Knox Press, 1998)

Gilleasbuig Macmillan, **A Workable Belief: thoughts on the Apostles' Creed**, (Edinburgh: Saint Andrew Press, 1993)

Frances Young, **The Making of the Creeds**, (London: SCM Press, 1991)

THINK

1. What do you find helpful or challenging in the Apostles' Creed?

2. Why do you think that each of its statements was included?

3. Where might creeds such as this be useful in the life of the Church?

ACT

Write your own short creed as a way of exploring your faith.

After the profession of belief in the Spirit there is a series of further Christian commitments of faith, concerning the universal Church, the communion of saints, the forgiveness of sins, the resurrection of the body, and eternal life. Under its three main headings, the Creed covers a fairly extensive range of the essentials of Christian faith. At the same time, it is not by any means comprehensive. For example, it does not offer any statement on the authority or inspiration of scripture, the sacraments of baptism and the Lord's Supper, or the understanding of the ministry of the Church. And there is nothing by way of ethical teaching in the Creed.

The need for such statements of the Christian faith arises at certain critical points in the life of the Church. One obvious moment is when a person is being instructed in the Christian faith. In the early Church this led to creeds being used in the sacrament of baptism, and here they are still sometimes used to the present day, as those undergoing or those presenting a child for baptism make a public confession of faith. But the Creed can also be used more widely by the Church – perhaps forming part of a regular service of worship or of a communion service, or perhaps offering a way of identifying to non-Christians some of the basic features of Christian faith. ■

My Story Fiona Marks

I grew up in a tiny village in Perthshire called Errol and one of my earliest memories of church was being given a sixpence for the collection and then my brother and I nipping into the post office, which was open to sell the Sunday newspapers, spending threepence on sweets and putting the remaining threepence in the collection!

From childhood to adulthood, I vacillated between having a sneaking suspicion that God was real but then finding lots of ways to explain away his possible existence. As a music student at the RSAMD in Glasgow, I used to ask the students in the Christian Union lots of questions about God when I thought no-one else was listening ... Did they *really* believe God existed? Did they actually talk to him? How could they possibly believe Jesus was real?

Three wonderful kids and the devastation of a broken marriage later, I was a single mum struggling to make ends meet, still fascinated by the God question but still sceptical.

As a professional musician, I regularly went into local care homes to provide volunteer entertainment for the residents. I played for two lovely ladies who sang on those occasions, who happened to be Christians. We had lots of chats back and forth about faith and life, and all the while I was watching them and the way they lived their lives, almost without realising I was doing it.

I remember being struck that they seemed to love me unequivocally, just as I was, without ever judging me. They used to bring me food parcels and huge boxes of washing powder and one time, as I emptied the box they had left, I found a large bottle of Paris perfume at the bottom – the most extravagant luxury in the midst of the essentials, which made me weep uncontrollably.

A few weeks later, they suggested I visit my local church. Not wanting to offend after all their kindness, we trooped along. It was astonishing – I recognised the same love and peace there which I felt from my singing friends. I was invited to an Alpha Supper a few weeks later, to which I responded, 'I'd love to come – what is it?', sensing even then that I 'belonged' in that atmosphere. I found answers to many questions on the Alpha course I subsequently attended and, 20 years later, I'm happy to shout from the rooftops that God is indeed gloriously real!

I BELIEVE IN JESUS CHRIST

Donald MacEwan
University Chaplain, University of St Andrews

The longest section in the Apostles' Creed is about Jesus Christ. This makes sense: after all, Christians are named after Christ, and in some ways it is belief in Jesus Christ (statements about Jesus and trust in him) which distinguishes Christians from people of other faiths or philosophies of life. Candidates for baptism and/or confirmation are asked:

*Do you believe in Jesus Christ,
your Saviour and Lord?
They reply:
I believe in Jesus Christ,
God's only Son, our Lord,
who was conceived by the Holy Spirit,
born of the Virgin Mary,
suffered under Pontius Pilate,
was crucified, died, and was buried;
he descended to the dead.
On the third day he rose again;
he ascended into heaven,
he is seated
at the right hand of the Father,
and he will come to judge
the living and the dead.*

In this section we will make it as far as 'suffered under Pontius Pilate'.

Jesus Christ

Jesus is his name. Names almost always matter in the Bible. Jesus means 'The Lord saves' (*The Lord is* the way the Bible in English represents the Hebrew name for God). Both Mary and Joseph were told by the angel, before Mary's child was born, to name him Jesus. This meaning is picked up in the question which candidates are asked, 'Do you believe in Jesus Christ, your *Saviour* and Lord?' And it also reflects the meaning of God's forgiving grace, rescuing us from the wrong turnings we take that we explored earlier.

'Christ', although it looks like a surname, is not a family name. Rather it is the English form of the Greek word for 'Messiah'. In the Bible, God promises to his people Israel that he will be their God and is committed to being their deliverer – their Messiah. Throughout Jesus' life people wondered if he was the Messiah and following his death his followers became increasingly convinced that this was the case. They realised that in Jesus, God had fulfilled his promise. And so when Christians say they trust in Jesus Christ, they affirm that the promise of God found throughout the Old Testament – his calling of a people to be his people, his commitment to love them, his promise to be their king – has reached its fruition in Jesus, a Jewish man. As Peter, Jesus' disciple, says at the end of his sermon in Jerusalem just days following Jesus' ascension:

> 'Therefore let the entire house of Israel know with certainty that God has made him both Lord and Messiah, this Jesus whom you crucified.' (Acts 2:36)

God's only Son

Christians do not only believe that Jesus is a Jewish man, anointed by God. They also trust in Jesus as God's only Son. Now, just as *Father* is such a common image for God that we can overlook the meaning contained in it, so too with *Son*. Of course, a son is a male child, offspring of parents. Jesus has a mother – Mary – and as for a father, Christians believe that Jesus' father is God the Holy Spirit. This has helped Christians see that Jesus is both human and divine, both fully human and fully God. Being *Son of God* is a way of saying that Jesus

The word *only* in the phrase 'God's only Son' has a slightly vulnerable feel. And this is deliberate, for it echoes one of the most famous Bible verses:

> 'For God so loved the world that he gave his only Son, so that everyone who believes in him may not perish but may have eternal life.' (John 3:16)

The only could refer to the possibility that God had other children not given for the world. But in the absence of any other children, the sense of God's self-giving becomes clear. In giving his only Son, God essentially gives himself. He did not hold back a part of himself. He did not retain a part of himself untouched by his self-giving, an inner core of safety.

Our Lord

If *God's only Son* refers to Jesus' relationship with God, then *our Lord* refers to his relationship with us. Few of us today have a human lord, on whose land we live and to whom we owe a proportion of our property on a feudal basis. We resist anybody or any institution that attempts to lord it over us. But even if the language feels old-fashioned, the concept is strikingly contemporary. For our lives are all lived according to one principle or another. It could be work which demands ever more hours, or the needs of our family; it could be our appearance which leads us to spend hours in the gym or before the mirror; it could be

" Jesus means 'The Lord saves'

is God. The New Testament inches its way towards this conclusion, though it tends to do so by means of historical narrative, stories and argument in letters rather than clear theological statement. Furthermore, when we look at the Holy Spirit in a later section (page 36), we will find a third way in which Christians refer to God, which has led to the understanding of God as Trinity, Father, Son and Holy Spirit.

the desire to have the latest thing, to not miss out, to keep up in status. In other words, we all have a lord or multiple lords, even if we don't call them that. Christians trust in Jesus Christ as our Lord. It is his kingdom we serve. It is his principles we live by. It is his love we share. The Apostles' Creed runs to about twenty lines – it's pretty brief. But the shortest creed in the Bible is only three words: 'Jesus is Lord' (Romans 10:9).

Who was conceived by the Holy Spirit

This is another way of saying that Jesus is the Son of God, that he had no human biological father – though he was brought up by Joseph. When the angel Gabriel announced the news to Mary that she would conceive a child, Mary queried this as she was a virgin. The angel replied:

> 'The Holy Spirit will come upon you, and the power of the Most High will overshadow you; therefore the child to be born will be holy; he will be called Son of God.' (Luke 1:35)

And so it is also a way of showing that God was involved in this birth and life, so deeply involved that his own self was found in the conception. The making flesh of God – the incarnation – was not some airy waving of a divine hand, some plucking of a random individual to bear the weight of God's presence. It was God himself sharing created form, from implantation in the womb until death and beyond. This is the first mention of the Holy Spirit in the Creed, and indicates that God is not ultimately separable into three constituent parts. As the Holy Spirit, God is active in creation and in Jesus, and we shall look at belief in the Holy Spirit in more detail later.

There is a miracle here – human birth requires a human father. And so some Christians have struggled with this aspect of the Creed. As we noted earlier, faith often lives alongside doubt, and some Christians are more prone than others to question the miraculous conception of Jesus today. All I hope to do here is to help explore what it could mean to trust in Jesus Christ, conceived by the Holy Spirit.

Born of the Virgin Mary

These words get to the heart of the incarnation: the Son of God, yet born to a human mother, in a specific place, Bethlehem, at a specific time, just over 2,000 years ago. The mention of Mary in the Creed brings home to us the involvement of the creaturely, the human in the purposes of God. God did not stride over the earth in a human disguise to teach us his purpose. Rather, God entered creaturely life, born of a human mother, becoming human flesh, God with us, good news, bearing in himself the gift of peace and joy.

The stories of angels, shepherds and wise men move and delight us. But they contain within them the germ of what will follow: Mary's pain at the suffering she would face in her son's death; and the gift of myrrh, a spice for embalming a dead body.

Suffered under Pontius Pilate

What a jump! The Apostles' Creed moves in one short phrase from his birth to the day of his death. For his suffering under Pontius Pilate – the beating and mocking by Roman soldiers, the humiliation of his arrest, trial and verdict – happened just a few hours before he was put to death on a cross. But what happened in the thirty or so years in between? Isn't the life of Jesus important? What does the comma cover?

His life does matter. One reason the Creed is silent is because many details of his life are recounted in the gospels, and were not controversial in the early centuries of the Church. Another is because his birth, death and resurrection were understood as being so crucial for our salvation that, by contrast, his life seemed less significant. But it was not. The four gospels recount events during these years which help us understand who Jesus was. He was baptised in the River Jordan, apparently taking on his role as the one who would represent all human beings. He was tempted by the devil, but resisted, trusting in God, to whom he frequently prayed. He healed people, gave sight to the blind and hearing to the deaf, cured them of illness and banished conditions of the mind. He raised the dead to life. He preached the coming of the kingdom, and called people to follow him. Twelve whom he called to be his followers, his disciples, are named. He taught, sometimes directly, often by means of stories called parables which used everyday situations his hearers would understand to cast light on to the deepest realities of life and of his kingdom. He was compassionate to many, critical of some – usually those in authority and often religious leaders.

He raised the dead to life.

READ

Luke 1:1–23:32 read the gospel according to Luke

Stephen Cottrell *et al.*, **Pilgrim: turning to Christ**, (London: Church House Publishing, 2013)

Francis Spufford, **Unapologetic: why, despite everything, Christianity can still make surprising emotional sense**, (London: Faber and Faber, 2012) Section 5

Rowan Williams, **Tokens of Trust: an introduction to Christian belief**, (Norwich: Canterbury Press, 2007) Section 3

Tom Wright, **Simply Christian**, (London: SPCK Publishing, 2011) Section 7

Tom Wright, **Simply Jesus**, (London: SPCK Publishing, 2011) Sections 6–12

THINK

1. How important to you are the lines of the Creed, 'conceived by the Holy Spirit, born of the Virgin Mary'?

2. Why do you think Jesus healed people?

3. Why do you think Jesus suffered?

ACT

What would acting as a disciple mean in your life – what would have to change, and what would stay the same?

In short, his life as the Messiah was one in which God's reign began to be seen and felt and lived by those around Jesus. He was not the Messiah they may have wanted, who by force of arms would cast out the Roman lords (such as Pontius Pilate, Roman governor in Judea, representing the Emperor). But he was the Messiah in whom God was found, speaking truth, spreading justice, bringing healing, sharing peace and defeating death. He formed a community of people shaped by their trust in him.

It is this man, Son of God, son of Mary, who suffered under Pontius Pilate, whose life brought forth such rejection. Following an encounter which we call the Transfiguration, in which Jesus hears the voice of God, he turns towards Jerusalem, the centre of the Jewish nation, in which the Temple stood, where earth and heaven met, where his people encountered God. He seems to know that there he will encounter opposition, violence and death. And so it proves: he objects publicly to corruption in the Temple, which leads to the Jewish religious authorities seeking a way to silence him. He shares a last supper with his disciples, following which he is betrayed by Judas, arrested in the Garden of Gethsemane, denied by Peter, tried before both Jewish and Roman courts, and found guilty, probably of blasphemy and of claiming to be King. The punishment is execution, before which he is beaten and mocked. All this is found in the single phrase, *suffered under Pontius Pilate*. ■

WHY IS THERE SUFFERING?

Kathy Galloway
Head of Christian Aid Scotland

People often ask about Christianity, 'If God is a God of love, why is there so much suffering in the world?' Or, 'Why do bad things happen to good people?' And when trouble strikes in individual lives, the despairing question may be, 'Why me? What have I done to deserve this?'

Theologians and pastors have wrestled with these big questions for centuries. The Psalms are full of them; even Jesus cried, 'My God, my God, why have you forsaken me?'

But in my work with Christian Aid, which, along with its partners, is engaged in the relief of pain and injustice across the world, I find my response is shaped by two themes running side by side in the gospel accounts of Jesus' suffering and death. One is a theme of *presence and compassion*; the other a theme of *absence and silence*.

The first is the story of those who loved Jesus. Many women had followed him from Galilee and provided for him. Now they accompanied him on the way of the cross and watched from a distance as he suffered his terrible agony and death. The good men Nicodemus and Joseph of Arimathea (himself wrapping Jesus' body in a linen sheet and laying him in his own tomb) gave of their wealth so that Jesus might have a decent burial according to custom. John, the beloved disciple, and Mary, the mother of Jesus, gave comfort to one another. The women from Galilee wept together, and watched where Jesus was laid, not forgetting the practical tasks of preparing spices and ointments, and probably preparing food. And Mary Magdalene waited and mourned. After the crucifixion, all of them observed the Sabbath, doing what was necessary for life to go on.

This story of just being there alongside people, doing ordinary, vital practical things, is one that I hear constantly as Christian Aid partners support communities who have lost everything, including loved ones, in natural disasters, wars and conflicts; in times of drought, failed crops and hunger; and through terrible health crises, like Ebola, HIV/AIDS or malaria. Presence and compassion cares for the whole person and engages the whole community.

But being alongside people in suffering does not only happen in poor countries. It happens wherever people watch with others through long nights, prepare food for those too weary or ill to do it themselves, look after the children, get the shopping in, read to a friend or simply offer an encouraging word or smile or shoulder to lean on. It happens when people respect one another's wishes, honour their confidences, protect their need for privacy, and refrain from telling them how to solve their problems or live their lives. This ministry of presence and compassion is perhaps the best flowering of our mutual humanity.

And yet at its heart is a kind of powerlessness. It is the powerlessness of our own inadequacy and frailty in the face of the deep hurt of others. It is the powerlessness of watching someone we love die. It is the powerlessness of people in the face of a catastrophically unjust world economic order which puts massive, unquantifiable resources into protecting the interests and profits of the powerful of the world and almost nothing by comparison into overcoming poverty and preventable or treatable disease. It is the powerlessness of being confronted with physical and spiritual violence at every level. For Christian Aid, it is the powerlessness of knowing all that we cannot do or save, in spite of our best efforts. We all stand powerless at the foot of the cross.

Presence and compassion are needed in the face of suffering and death. But ultimately, where Jesus went, his friends could not follow. Suffering is also a story of loss and absence. None of us can really know what the reality of suffering is for another, even if that other is Jesus. In the mystery of human suffering, the other truthful response, along with compassion, is silence.

To keep silent is not to minimise or disrespect another's suffering, far less to be complacent in the face of it. We are not thereby relieved of the need to keep working to overcome all that causes preventable suffering. It is simply to recognise that suffering and death is part of the human condition, about which we have many theories or theologies, all of which are ultimately inadequate. Some of them are bleak indeed.

We who are Christians give a special meaning to the suffering and death of Jesus. The cross is a reminder of suffering, loss and grief. It is a symbol of all that the worst of human violence and fear can do to goodness and innocence. The Apostles' Creed tells us that after he was crucified, Jesus descended into hell. The descent into hell for each of us may be a journey into the depths of our own potential for violence and corruption, into our nameless imaginings and our darkest fears of punishment, betrayal, abandonment and the terror of the unknown, into the destruction of all life and love.

" just being there alongside people

But Christ went to hell for us, and so there is nowhere in life or in death that is not God-encompassed; nowhere that is beyond the power of love to reach and touch; nothing and no one that is beyond redemption and the possibility of new life. 'Why do you look for him among the dead?' the angel asked. 'He is not here. He is alive.' God in Jesus dares to place love above time. The confession of the faith that 'he descended into hell, and on the third day he rose again from the dead' points to this awesome truth. ∎

READ

C. S. Lewis, **A Grief Observed**, (London: Faber and Faber, 2013)

Philip Yancey, **Where Is God When It Hurts?**, (Michigan: Zondervan, 1997)

Nick Baines, **Scandal of Grace** (Edinburgh: Saint Andrew Press, 2008)

Kathy Galloway, **Walking in Darkness and Light**: **sermons and reflections** (Edinburgh: Saint Andrew Press, 2001)

THINK

1. What might Christ's call to take up one's cross and follow him mean?

2. What role can Christians play in the suffering of the world?

3. Consider the way in which God is experienced as both *presence* and *absence*. What does this mean for human beings who suffer? What does this mean to you?

ACT

Think of someone you know who is suffering – what is a way that you could be present with them, or show them compassion?

www.christianaid.org.uk/scotland

DEATH AND RESURRECTION

Donald MacEwan
University Chaplain, University of St Andrews

This section will look at what Christians believe about Jesus' death, burial, resurrection, ascension and return. These lines of the Creed are the centre of our faith.

Was crucified, died and was buried

Jesus suffered under Pontius Pilate, but he was also crucified upon his order, an event we recall on Good Friday. Why did Jesus die?

There are historical reasons. To the Romans, and their emperor, Caesar, any threat to their empire was better snuffed out. To the Jewish authorities, Jesus' appeal to the people, his radical call to discipleship, his subversion of Temple practices was dangerous. It was Passover, a season in Jerusalem when the population was swelled by pilgrims, and the atmosphere was tense. Jesus entered a Jerusalem in which too many powerful people feared that if he were allowed to continue, their status would be threatened. And so he was publicly executed on a cross, between two criminals.

But for those exploring the Christian faith, rather than reconstructing historical motives, there is another set of answers to the question *Why did Jesus die?* This question can be rephrased even more starkly: *Why did God allow Jesus to die?*

Here we return again to the theme explored in the section that asks, 'What is a Christian?' (page 6): confessing our need of God's forgiving grace. Jesus' death is the means by which God's forgiving grace is offered to the world. Now, forgiveness does not suddenly appear in the scriptures with the crucifixion of Jesus. The Old Testament describes a number of ways by which God's people seek to make themselves right with God. There are sacrifices, of grain and animals. There are laws to obey. There is justice to observe. But with the benefit of hindsight these approaches now seem like a preparation for the ultimate way which God offers forgiveness to the world: the gift of his Son.

Why did God allow Jesus to die?

Jesus tells a parable which may help us understand:

> A man planted a vineyard, and leased it to tenants, and went to another country for a long time. When the season came, he sent a slave to the tenants in order that they might give him his share of the produce of the vineyard; but the tenants beat him and sent him away empty-handed. Next he sent another slave; that one also they beat and insulted and sent away empty-handed. And he sent still a third; this one also they wounded and threw out. Then the owner of the vineyard said, 'What shall I do? I will send my beloved son; perhaps they will respect him.' But when the tenants saw him, they discussed it among themselves and said, 'This is the heir; let us kill him so that the inheritance may be ours.' So they threw him out of the vineyard and killed him. (Luke 20:9–15)

The Church has traditionally understood this parable as referring to God's relationship with his people. The three slaves represent the previous ways God reached out to his people, inviting a faithful response from them, but encountering rebellion instead. On the final occasion, the landlord sends his son, but he too is killed – a seeming reference in the parable to Jesus himself.

But why would God need to send his own son? Could rescue not have come some less expensive way? Yet the costliness of this gift reflects the costliness of the sin of the world. As you read this, think over the events of the last week or month in the news – consider the violence perpetrated by individuals, terrorists, armed forces and governments. Or think of situations known to you – consider the unhappiness caused by human actions or inactions, speech or silence. Or recall your own life – consider the reality of your own relationships, motives and thoughts. I imagine you are all too aware of the cost of human self-centredness, or our own self-centredness. All too often, sorrow, pain, suffering and even death are the result.

If that is so, we may begin to see a reason, even a sort of logic, to the gift of God's only son. Given the never-ceasing love of God, which allows us freedom but longs to help us to choose the good, given the involvement of God in the world which he makes, sustains and is present in by his Son, how could that commitment not lead to a premature and humiliating death? Given the way the world's powers act, this presence of self-giving love, if truly committed, had to be extinguished. And the word *buried* in the Creed makes clear that Jesus was truly dead, and shared the fate of all humanity, beginning the journey beyond death to oblivion.

He descended to the dead

This line is better known in the older form of the Creed – *He descended into hell*. It emphasises his death, but indicates more. In the Orthodox Church, many churches feature an image of the dead Christ descending into hell for the purpose of bringing souls out, leading them into life with him. The descent into hell is a symbol, in a way, of salvation.

After all, how should the death of Jesus be understood as the means of God's forgiving grace? Here there are a variety of ways in which the Church has answered the question. Jesus represents humanity. Jesus is a substitute for the punishment humanity should rightly receive on account of its sin.

God pays a ransom (Jesus) to the devil for humanity. God defeats evil, death and the devil in the death and resurrection of Jesus. God satisfies the need for justice through this perfect sacrifice. The Bible itself provides a range of images and concepts by way of explanation, and it is a fascinating, sometimes mind-boggling question how to understand these and other approaches to this question. But trusting in God does not mean we have to know which solution is right. Christians differ, and sometimes acknowledge that here is a mystery we may never plumb the depths of completely. But what is true is that Jesus' death is the means by which our sins are forgiven and death is overcome, and that we are drawn by Jesus into life with him, reconciled with God.

On the third day he rose again

This is the very heart of the Christian faith which we are exploring. Easter, the principal day on which the resurrection is celebrated, is the most important day in the Christian year. First there was a discovery. Women followers of Jesus went to his tomb early on the Sunday morning (the third day if Good Friday is the first) to attend to his body which had been buried hastily on Friday. But they discovered the tomb was empty – Jesus' body was not there. This man, whose death they had witnessed, whose death had been confirmed by a soldier's spear, whose dead body had been buried, was missing.

But as well as an empty tomb, Jesus appeared to his followers. First to the women, then to Peter and other disciples. Some appearances are in Jerusalem where he died and was buried; others are in Galilee some 70 miles to the north where he had spent most of his life and ministry. He has a physical form: he speaks, he eats, he can be touched. But his body seems different from others (and from how he was before he died): he is not easily recognised, he can appear in a locked room, and he is not always with them. These appearances last for some 40 days.

What does this mean? Fundamentally it means and shows that God's love is stronger than death. God poured himself into the human situation in Jesus, the one who was conceived by the Holy Spirit, who suffered under Pontius Pilate. The world did its worst to Jesus, resulting in his death. Buried, he began a journey to oblivion. Without resurrection, he would be a half-remembered religious eccentric, known perhaps to a handful of scholars of Jewish history during the Roman Empire. But God's love, unconditionally faithful to his creation, proved stronger, infinitely so, than evil, violence, injustice and death. Death could not hold God's Messiah. The crucified one was raised by God from death.

It also reveals what we can be, given his love. We can share in this resurrection. All that is selfish, violent and deathly in our world and society need not be victorious. There is another possibility always open now, a future in which God's love is present, active, healing and offering hope. Within the Church, the resurrection of Jesus offers the prospect, indeed the gift of reconciliation. In the light of God raising Jesus from the dead, we do not need to live for ourselves within the Church, we do not need to maintain our differences, our petty squabbles, our pride, but instead we are able to be open to the spirit of Christ drawing us into unity and peace.

And the bodily resurrection of Jesus offers us the promise that our own lives too will not end in death, but will be open to the power of God beyond death, whose love will not give up on us, and who will provide from the riches of his grace the prospect of new life in the new creation.

He ascended into heaven,
he is seated
at the right hand of the Father.

The resurrection appearances came to an end. After 40 days, the New Testament records that Jesus was taken up, into heaven. It would be easy to think that this means Jesus has gone away, that the Son of God, albeit the resurrected Son of God, is no longer with us. But that is in fact exactly what the ascension does not mean. Heaven is part of God's creation, the realm from which he acts. For Jesus to be in heaven means, first that he is with God completely (*the right hand* is the place of honour, without any sense of separation), and second that he remains with the world. For with the ascension of Christ comes the descent of the Holy Spirit. God remains with us, working within the world, loving his people, reconciling creation. True, we do not see Christ in the way his first disciples did, but the resurrected Jesus said to his disciple Thomas, 'Have you believed because you have seen me? Blessed are those who have not seen and yet have come to believe' (John 20:29).

And he will come to judge
the living and the dead.

The Christian faith looks forward. In trusting in God as Creator, we believe in a God who made the universe, who set time and space in being, who accompanies creation in being, sustaining it moment by moment and who is drawing creation to its fulfilment. Sometimes it may feel as if this troubled world can never get any better, that the cycles of violence and revenge, pain and death will never be broken.

The Christian faith is in God who called creation good, and whose loving will for creation is for that goodness to be established and – in light of human sin – re-established in Jesus Christ. And so we hope in God that all the pain and sorrow of creaturely life, all the violence and injustice of the earth will be set right. Scripture envisages this fulfilment in many ways – the new creation, a new heaven and a new earth, the rule of God – and such a conclusion involves judgment. This is connected to the reign already begun in the coming of the Messiah, his teaching and community, his death and resurrection, reconciliation and grace.

Some of Jesus' parables seem to be about this final judgment, and make a strong distinction between those who will be accepted by God in the judgment, who will then be part of God's eternal reign, and those who will be found wanting, who will be outside God's kingdom. At other times the Bible seems to indicate that the whole creation will be brought under God's rule, that nothing and no-one will remain outside this new creation. It is significant to note that this hope, for God's setting right all the ways that creation was wronged, is grounded in the resurrection of Jesus. This is the act which offers evidence for this rescue, and hope that it has begun. ∎

READ

Matthew 21–27 Crucifixion (also in Mark, Luke and John)

Matthew 28; Mark 16; Luke 24; John 20–21 Resurrection

Acts 1:1–11 Ascension

Romans 8:18–39 The glory about to be revealed

Rowan Williams, **Tokens of Trust: an introduction to Christian belief**, (Norwich: Canterbury Press, 2007) Section 4

Rowan Williams, **Resurrection: interpreting the Easter Gospel**, (London: Darton, Longman & Todd, 2014)

Tom Wright, **Simply Christian**, (London: SPCK Publishing, 2011) Section 8

Tom Wright, **Simply Jesus**, (London: SPCK Publishing, 2011) Sections 13–15

THINK

1. Why do you think Jesus died?

2. Why do you think Jesus rose from the dead?

3. There is a hymn called 'Every morning is Easter morning from now on.' What do you think the writer had in mind?

ACT

How does the Christian belief that love is stronger than death affect *your* idea of life?

DOUBT

Dorothy Neilson
Life Coach

Doubt. It's just a word. Nothing more. But it whispers uncertainty and leaves us feeling empty, shaken and even sad. Doubt! Can it be true? Have I got it all wrong? It just doesn't seem possible any more. So what's gone wrong? Did I just imagine it all? Was there never a God in the first place? Did I make it all up in my head?

And the answer is ... Drum roll ... well ... there is no answer to these questions, I am sorry to say. But let us speculate further. What happens when we begin to have our doubts? And what is it all about?

There is a theory that makes a lot of sense to me that suggests that we go through different stages in our spiritual and faith journey in much the same way that we go through different stages of physical life. When we are children, we are little, cute, vulnerable and malleable. We grow up and become different.

And so in our spiritual life, we start at the beginning with stories and impressions which make sense to us and to our embryonic faith. It is all so simple. God is love. We know God because of knowing Jesus. I am loved by him. He is on my side. All is well with the world.

As we grow into our faith 'adolescence' we perhaps become a little more discerning. We grapple a bit more with the facts of what we believe and what we see as true. Sometimes we can become quite dogmatic and feel very sure of the truths of our faith. We tend to gather in groups of likeminded people and stay around other Christians who think as we do. Anyone with different ideas or beliefs might seem slightly dangerous to our minds.

These days of certainties may last forever for some of us. We never doubt; we never waver. We feel sure of these central beliefs and are satisfied with that. We are happy in our church, with our Christian friends and leadership and there is no reason to falter.

But for others, the spiritual equivalent of mid-life looms ominously on the horizon and it might feel like we begin to lose the plot.

This is the category that I come into. Having earnestly made up my mind about my theology in my teens and twenties, I was hit by the shockwaves of midlife. What had seemed so clear and so simple suddenly trembled and crumbled and I felt the emptiness and the abandonment of seeing my world with no God in charge, leaving me adrift and alone. I wasn't alone. There are many, many others who get washed away in the storm following midlife and find themselves washed-up on strange shores where they no longer hear the echoes of heaven and therefore feel bereft and lonely.

These folks are experiencing 'doubt'. And all we can hear in that dark place are our own voices, accusing ourselves of being too simplistic or accusing God of being totally unfair. This was not how it was supposed to be. God should not be like this. This isn't right. We believed, against all the odds, that God was good and that if we stuck by him, everything would be alright. We blame God. And we blame ourselves.

But as physical midlife moves into maturity, so we have a choice about our lives. Some just give up. Others re-evaluate. Some think there's no point in struggling with belief. We're too old. It's too late. We haven't got the energy. Another alternative is to hand over our doubts to God, and trust that God can still act in our lives. One way to do this is to begin to control our thinking about the problem; learn to sit with the questions. Settle into silence. Simply pray that God's presence will become real to us. Be still, for the presence of the Lord is all around you whether you believe it with your head, feel it in your bones or even if you just experience his still, quiet company.

Doubt need not have the last word. It can be part of the journey. ■

READ

Psalm 56 Trust in God under Persecution

Psalm 69 Prayer for Deliverance from Persecution

Psalm 71 Prayer for Lifelong Protection and Help

Richard Rohr, **Falling Upward: a spirituality for the two halves of life**, (London: SPCK Publishing, 2012)

Dorothy Jane Neilson, **Me, God and Prozac: tools for tough times**, (Yorkshire: Gilead Books, 2014)

Joyce Rupp, **Dear Heart, Come Home: path of mid-life spirituality**, (New York: Crossroad Publishing, 1996)

THINK

Write or tell of a time when you were shaken by doubt when you didn't know what you believed any more.

1. What might have brought on this experience?

2. What emotions did you feel at the time – angry, sad or frightened?

3. What did the experience teach you about yourself and/or God?

ACT

Why not start a journal to explore your thoughts on faith and doubt?

My Story Andrew McPherson

When I think on my Christian faith the following ideas come to mind: here; open; promise; and everlasting.

Here. God is always here for me. In my faith I have been aware of God's love being for me. It surrounds me and carries me on my way and demonstrates itself to others.

Open. God is always open. Just like he is always here, God is waiting to listen to us all the time, ready to comfort us and help us and others.

Promise. God's promise lives with us each and every day. His promise of all good things, of victory over death and of grace, to name a few things that give me a glow in my heart, a smile on my face and a bounce in my step whenever I need it.

Everlasting. God's love and presence is everlasting. I can depend on it forever and with whatever I give I will always receive more and I can only be thankful.

Here, Open, Promise and Everlasting. These are just four of the things that I take my hope from.

Hope is such a powerful part of the Christian faith; it can be felt in many ways and is demonstrated in the world around us. For me, hope ultimately comes from the resurrection of Jesus Christ. I see the resurrection as the cornerstone of the Christian faith: without it we would not have life and the assurances of life in faith with Christ. The resurrection gives us life here and now, and life ever after. This gives me hope for my everyday life and changes my perspective on the world around me.

Hope also relates to smaller things that happen in my life, such as when annoying or negative things happen. I can take hope in the promise that things can get better, and that this is all just part of the journey.

This hope has shaped me into who I am today, from the hope I take from God, from my friends, my family and others in my congregation. It has given me strength, and I am sure that I cannot be the only one. I can rely on my hope whenever I need to, and it has shown me who I am and who God is.

I BELIEVE IN THE HOLY SPIRIT

Donald MacEwan
University Chaplain, University of St Andrews

We started by looking at God the Father and Creator followed by Jesus Christ – the Son of God. Now we turn to God as Holy Spirit, and the further implications this has for the life of faith.

I believe in the Holy Spirit

God is the Holy Spirit. God is not part of creation, made of physical stuff which scientists can dissect. Yet God is certainly real. And, in our inadequate human language, we call God 'Spirit'. And this term Spirit is then used to express how God's own being is a being of love, and how God relates in love to creation. As Holy Spirit, God's love is shared.

Jesus, before his death and resurrection, promises that God will send his Spirit to be with his people. And then on the day of a Jewish festival called Shavuot in Hebrew and Pentecost in Greek, just after Jesus' ascension, the disciples who were gathered in Jerusalem felt God with them in a new way. This was a set of strange experiences: they saw tongues of fire over each of them; they felt a rushing wind; they could be understood by people in their own languages. Ever since, the church has understood this day as the coming of the Holy Spirit. Christians trust in God as Father, in Jesus as Lord and in the Holy Spirit as with them. What does it mean for God to be with us through his Spirit?

I think it means that we are supported, guided, challenged and inspired. This will be different for every reader, so let me give some examples which may find echoes in our own lives.

The Spirit supports us. For example, the Spirit in us helps, in the most devastating of times, our stomach lurching, our brains reeling, to hold on to a sense of meaning, to a community of love, and to the possibility that somehow, life will again be possible or even contain joy.

The Spirit guides us. For example, when considering a difficult decision, whether to commit to a relationship, despite misgivings, despite doubts over our characters, our different views on certain issues, fears over a future closed off – the Spirit of truth within us helps us come to make decisions, to make good judgments, to guide us in the often unclear path ahead.

The Spirit challenges us. For example, the Spirit may help us realise that we have hurt someone deeply by our actions, and that we need to be reconciled.

God will send his Spirit
to be with his people.

And the Spirit inspires us. For example, we may be inspired by the Spirit to give our time, energy and presence to a community project where we live, improving life for people in trouble.

Support, guidance, challenge and inspiration – just four ways the Spirit with and in us makes a radical difference to our lives. Believing in the Holy Spirit means trusting that God is with us in our lives, that nothing we do is without God's involvement, that no situation is without God's presence.

We have seen that the three sections of the Creed focus respectively on God the Father, Son and Holy Spirit. When the early Christians reflected on their experience of the activity of Father, Son and Holy Spirit in creation, reconciliation and presence, they coined a new term to describe the God whom they encountered: they spoke of God as *Trinity*. The importance of this term was to insist that Father, Son and Holy Spirit were not three separate gods, but one God, known and active in three distinct ways of being God. The new word helped to emphasise how unfamiliar this idea really was, how it broke open the old patterns of having either one single God or many different gods. Trusting in God who is Father, Son and Holy Spirit, a Trinity of love, is what makes Christian belief Christian.

The rest of the third section looks as if it is descriptions of the Holy Spirit, but that's not quite right. In fact, it gives a brief list of some of God's gifts, which come from God's love as Father, Son and Holy Spirit. It does not include every gift of God – the Apostles' Creed doesn't try to cover every question an enquirer may have – but they are all gifts which matter. Let's look at them in turn.

The holy catholic Church

The Church doesn't always seem like a gift. There are beautiful churches, but also some damp, dusty barns. There are churches whose people are welcoming, understanding and full of integrity, but also churches whose people are narrow, unthinking and hypocritical. In any given church there may be all kinds of people. Indeed, a Christian may have all sorts of virtues and vices within their one person. Why should we believe in the Church?

The clue is in the adjectives. It is *holy* because of God's action in Christ. It is God's gift. It is more than a gathering of like-minded people, more even than an assembly of believers. It is the people God has called to worship him, to be shaped by the life of Jesus, to be supported, guided, challenged and inspired by the Holy Spirit. It is, fundamentally, a people who trust in Jesus. And so the holy Church, when it truly reflects the love of God, is where and how God's love is shared with the world, from the offering of God's forgiveness to our friends to the empowering of God's reign in justice and peace throughout our society.

And it is *catholic*. It is open with God's openness. Of course, *Catholic* sometimes refers to a particular branch of the Church – the Roman Catholic Church. But in fact the term means the broad sweep of God's openness, welcoming his children from every continent and culture, of every age and shape, every language and experience. The Church of Scotland participates in this catholic Church, alongside brothers and sisters from Ireland and Ethiopia, Africa and Arkansas, Rome and Russia, all praying, singing and serving in countless different ways.

The communion of saints

If the holy catholic Church speaks of a breadth in place, the communion of saints speaks of breadth across time. It represents the belief that Christians who have died are not lost to the Church, or gone from our community of faith, but are part of one and the same body. It's not an idea which has been much developed in the Church of Scotland, although we do reverence saints, often have our churches named after them and celebrate St Andrew's Day. It may be that as you read this you are conscious of those people in your lives who have passed on their faith to you, who have died and who perhaps belong to the communion of saints – the severe faces in a small, yellowed photograph; the grandmother who would take you to church; the teacher who patiently taught the Lord's Prayer; the friend whose faith stayed firm even as illness took hold. We do not enquire about God without some sort of cause. Christians are part of a communion of saints, 'so great a cloud of witnesses' as the New Testament book of Hebrews puts it, at 12:1. And we do not believe in isolation, rather we believe in this communion: a heritage we receive, and in which we participate, and which we in our turn pass on.

The forgiveness of sins

Again, the gift of God. We've already explored forgiveness when considering the question candidates for membership are asked – *Do you ... confess your need of God's forgiving grace?* And we returned to it when exploring the death of Jesus – as the means by which our rescue comes, our sins are forgiven. But perhaps here it is worth reflecting how fundamental the forgiveness of sins is in the Christian faith. It is not only the gift of God to those in need of rescue, it is the gift of those who are forgiven to each other.

The Church which is holy and catholic is a Church marked by this gift of forgiveness one to another. When a Church calls itself a Church, but its members are closed to each other, unforgiving, nursing grudges, content in resentments, it is as if it has a great hollow space within the brittle spun-sugar of its public face. If Jesus died for our forgiveness, and we are the people shaped by his life, death and resurrection, then we will be a community which lives in forgiveness. Not believing in the forgiveness of sins is tantamount to not trusting in God at all.

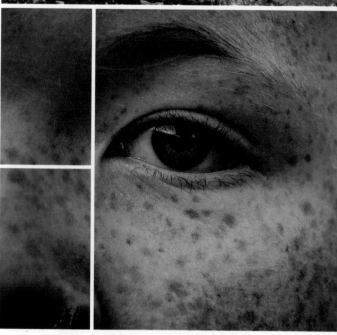

There are two places in the Bible where this is made very clear. The first is the Lord's Prayer, when Jesus teaches us to pray, *Forgive us our sins, as we forgive those who sin against us* (Matthew 6:12). We usually use the language of debts and debtors, or trespasses and those who trespass against us. The two are inescapably linked: God's setting things right must lead to our seeking to set things right. God's setting aside the dishonour of our sins must lead to our seeking to set aside our pride when we feel wronged.

And the other Bible story which matters here is a parable Jesus told, of the unforgiving servant. In this story, a man is forgiven a great debt, yet immediately demands a tiny sum owed him, and will not forgive it. Jesus is clear: the man who received mercy should have shown mercy (Matthew 18:21–35).

The resurrection of the body,
and the life everlasting.

The Christian faith is trust in God whose love never gives up, who continues to reach out to his creation to offer rescue when we become lost, to set things right which have gone wrong. Such a trust in such a love leads us to believe and to hope that this love does not give up even in death.

When people die there is a temptation to belittle it, to say that death is nothing of consequence, that it is a blip, a brief gap in the progress of life. But the Christian faith doesn't take this line – instead it takes death with complete seriousness. The Bible expresses human grief at the death of loved ones over and over again. David laments the death of Saul the king and Jonathan, his son and David's friend. Jesus weeps at the death of his friend Lazarus. Mary Magdalene is distraught at Jesus' death and the seeming loss of his body. God's suffering is seen most deeply in giving up his Son to death.

Death is the last enemy, the ultimate sign of a world gone wrong. But our hope is in God whose love is found even in death. The resurrection of Jesus is the action of God present in the death of his Son, his love not giving up in the face of death, but ultimately overcoming the worst that can be thrown in the face of love. He was raised in his body, as we explored earlier. His rising offers us a model and a means for our rising, for the resurrection of the body.

Of course we cannot know how this will take place. Every year as a university chaplain I spend an hour with first year medical students as they encounter for the first time the dead bodies they will be using to learn human anatomy. The Christian faith does not declare that these actual bodies will become alive again. But we do trust that God knows each person, and will, as the Bible says, clothe each person with a spiritual body, when this decaying world is set to rights. Christians hope in God who will bring heaven and earth to its true fulfilment. Jesus' life, death and resurrection began that, and his coming to judge the living and the dead are the conclusion of that same hope.

It is odd, perhaps, that the word heaven does not come in here. It was there at the start – *creator of heaven and earth* – but not in these closing words. Certainly, the sense of life beyond death is conveyed in the phrase the *life everlasting* (as well as *the communion of saints*). But *everlasting* captures only a hint of what such life might be. Simply going on and on is not necessarily a thing to relish. But eternal life can be understood as life with God, in perfect love, with fullness of life, with all that is lost restored, all that is damaged healed, all that is unfulfilled fulfilled.

Amen
A Hebrew word to end a prayer, like a signature below a letter which says *Yes, I have written this*, or *So be it. Amen* at the end of the Apostles' Creed perhaps means *Yes, this is what I believe – yes, I trust in God, yes, for all that I am exploring, for all that I am not completely sure, for all that I have moments or months of doubting – yes, I believe.* ■

READ

Acts 2:1–4, 37–39 Day of Pentecost

John 14:15–17, 25–26 The Spirit dwells within us

Galatians 5:22–23 The Spirit makes us more like Jesus

1 Corinthians 12–13 Gifts in the church, and the way of love

1 Corinthians 15 Resurrection of the dead

John Baillie, **And the Life Everlasting**, (Oxford: Oxford University Press, 1934)

Tom Wright, **Simply Christian**, (London: SPCK Publishing, 2011) Sections 9 & 10

Rowan Williams, **Tokens of Trust: An Introduction to Christian Belief**, (Norwich: Canterbury Press, 2007) Section 6

THINK

1. Support, guidance, challenge and inspiration – how do you believe the Holy Spirit is active in your life?

2. Do you feel you belong to a Church which is broad in space and broad in time? How?

3. In his book, *The Christian Experience of Forgiveness*, H. R. Mackintosh made the point that being certain of forgiveness is the secret at the heart of Christian faith. Do you feel that it is too much of a secret?

ACT

Try praying – ask God to reveal the presence of the Holy Spirit in you, around you and in others.

My Story Anne Smith

I was born and brought up in the Kirk. As a young married woman with small children I continued in faith but began to feel depressed, fearful and anxious. Not long after these feelings began I started to suffer from panic attacks. It was around this same time that the Holy Spirit began to become real to me.

At a point of real desperation and reaching the end of myself, the Holy Spirit came to me like water flowing into me, filling and renewing; giving me words to help encourage and inspire me, messages from God to me. In that moment I found an acceptance and experienced such an intensity of God's love deep within that nothing was ever quite the same again.

The Spirit took my childhood faith and deepened it and expanded it – though often hindered by my continued need for self-reliance. He brought scripture alive and showed me truths about God and Jesus I had not seen before; he brought healing into my life.

I have learned that only in the Spirit can I begin to aspire to a life which produces the fruit of the Spirit. As I have learned about the supernatural gifts, I have been able to use some of them with the Spirit's guidance and empowering.

Through the Holy Spirit my awareness of the holiness of God deepened and has led me into more meaningful worship and prayer, which has reinforced to me the indivisibility of the Trinity: Father, Son and Holy Spirit. When worshiping the Father – the Son and the Spirit are there; when walking and talking with Jesus – the Father and the Spirit are with us; when aware of the Spirit – the Father and the Son are close. At a particular time my focus may be on one but all are God, the three in one.

Today, the Spirit continues to highlight scriptures to me and show me opportunities to help others. The Spirit inspires and resources – often in a very practical way – helping me play my part in the kingdom of God. He continues to draw me alongside others and allows me to walk with them for part of their faith journey.

It is the Holy Spirit who gives me the quiet confidence of my faith, the assurance of God's love for me and the certainty of eternal life.

Whenever I am in tune with the Spirit, there is a sense of excitement, anticipation, a lightness in my spirit, and endless possibilities, and I give thanks that God's desire is for me to be in this amazing relationship with God: Father, Son and Holy Spirit.

FAITH AND SCIENCE

Andrew Torrance
Postdoctoral Research Fellow, University of St Andrews

For so many people in Scotland, there is an 'either-or' choice to be made between belief in God and reliance upon science. Even when people are willing to move past this assumption, they often end up with the view that science and Christianity are non-competitive because they concern two very different spheres: Christianity concerns a person's own particular worldview while science concerns the reality of the external world. As such, we see a particular compartmentalisation of science and faith.

So how can we recover an appreciation for the fact that the Christian message concerns the real world, which is also the arena for the sciences? How can the Church help people to recognise that there is a positive relationship between science and Christianity?

Before responding to these questions, there is another question to ask: why is it so important to integrate the perspective of the sciences with the exploration of faith?

A basic answer to this question is that our understanding of God's creation is massively informed by the insights of the natural sciences. Also, so much of what we know about what it means to be human is informed by modern science. Furthermore, scientific developments have proved fundamental to our understanding of what it means for us to function as a community that looks after one another and takes care of its natural environment. Yet so often Churches are isolated from the developments of contemporary science. Indeed, it is becoming increasingly difficult for the sciences to find a place within conversations in the Church. This has undoubtedly contributed to the perception that there is an either-or choice to be made between science and faith.

Another reason for this lack of integration is that scientists in the Church rarely have the chance to contribute their expertise to conversations in the Church. At the same time, popular 'scientific' voices outside the church are challenging the warrant for Christianity. This is particularly evident in the writings of the 'four horsemen' of new atheism: Richard Dawkins, Sam Harris, Daniel Dennett and Christopher Hitchens. This challenge, however, is not only coming from a handful of well-known atheists; it is evident right across society, in film and literature, popular journalism and social media.

One does not need to look far to see how much society has taken in the view that there is a serious tension, or even essential incompatibility, between Christianity and modern science. The more Christians hear their faith being ridiculed in the name of 'science', the more likely they are to avoid science, approach science defensively, or begin to deviate from the central tenets of their faith.

In turn, the more Christians seem ignorant of science, and the more that some popular Christian voices publicly denounce contemporary science, the more it seems to the secular world that Christianity is intellectually naive. All this creates another turn in the spiral of disengagement between the Church and the scientific world.

This downward spiral is so easily challenged by giving scientists, *as scientists*, a role to play in the mission of the Church. Many scientists in the Church – such as John Polkinghorne and Alister McGrath – have thought hard about how their vocation relates to their life of faith. Yet few of them have had the opportunity to help foster a constructive dialogue about science and faith. As such, these scientists have been present in Churches as a vital but often latent resource for helping to create an environment where science and faith can be seen to have a positive relationship.

By inviting scientists to contribute their expertise to the life of the Church, there is incredible potential for creating a conversation that will not only be stimulating for the congregation but also for the surrounding community. The Church will also have the opportunity to repudiate the myth that science has made the Church redundant and, at the same time, demonstrate that the Church is a centre for meaningful intellectual dialogue.

In the midst of this conversation, the gospel can be proclaimed in ways that could prove highly fruitful for the mission of all Churches: particularly to those who are sceptical about the notion of a positive relationship between science and Christianity. ■

> scientific developments have proved fundamental to our understanding of what it means for us to function as a community that looks after one another and takes care of its natural environment.

READ

www.scientistsincongregations.org

www.srtp.org.uk

www.jamesgregory.org.uk

David Fergusson, **Creation,** (Michigan: Eerdmans, 2014)

Alister and Joanna Collicutt McGrath, **The Dawkins Delusion?**, (London: SPCK Publishing, 2007)

Ruth Bancewicz, **God in the Lab: How Science Enhances Faith,** (Oxford: Monarch Books, 2015)

THINK

1. How does a theological account of creation relate to a scientific theory of the world?

2. How do scientific thinking and Christian thinking relate?

3. What does it mean for a scientist to take Jesus' miracles seriously?

ACT

Visit the Science in Congregations website and explore further the relationship between faith and science.

MEMBER'S VOW

Do you promise to join regularly
with your fellow Christians
in worship on the Lord's Day?

Do you promise
to be faithful in reading the Bible
and in prayer?

Do you promise
to give a fitting proportion
of your time, talents, and money
for the Church's work in the world?

Do you promise,
depending on the grace of God,
to profess publicly your loyalty to Jesus Christ,
to serve him in your daily work,
and to walk in his ways all the days of your life?

WHAT?

THINKING ABOUT BAPTISM

Donald MacEwan
University Chaplain, University of St Andrews

When people in the first days of the church believed in Jesus as their Lord they were baptised. It was the sign of God's forgiving grace, of their faith, and of their membership of Christ's body. As the Church became established in society, it grew less through new conversions and more through the birth of children to Christians. Households had been baptised in the earliest days of the Church, and now the infant children of believers were baptised. This was still a sign of God's forgiving grace, and still a sign of their belonging to Christ's body, but the faith was that of their parents who promised to bring their children up in the faith, passing it on. In time, it was hoped and intended, the baptised child would come to a mature faith, and share in communion.

Today, only a minority of infants in Scotland are baptised. The Church of Scotland does baptise infants, usually the children of members who promise to bring up their children in the life and worship of the Church. In today's largely secular society, many people become Christians at a later age, and thus before they are baptised. Their situation is more like the first days of the church rather than Scotland sixty years ago. And so when these people are baptised they are adults. Unlike infants, they confess their own faith.

To join the Church of Scotland you must be baptised. Perhaps you were baptised in a different church – the Roman Catholic Church or another Protestant church for example, as a baby or as a believer. The Church of Scotland accepts the baptism of other Churches, performed in the name of God, Father, Son and Holy Spirit. Many people, then, who join the Church having been baptised as infants do so in a service which *confirms* the faith into which their parents baptised them. They are saying that they have come to accept the faith of their baptism.

Others are baptised and confirmed in one and the same service, having never been baptised as children. Having come to faith, they want to mark their newly-found trust in God, show others that they are now Christians, and they do this by being baptised. There are slight differences in the wording of the profession of faith if baptism is involved, but the Apostles' Creed is common to both. The next section will look

at confirmation in more detail, while we'll think about baptism for the rest of this section. What happens when someone is baptised? The words of the service make clear its significance.

'Our baptism is the sign of dying to sin and rising to new life in Christ. ' (Common Order, p. 98) It is a moment between before and after, which marks the shift from the old life to the new life. The biblical picture of baptism by full immersion, going beneath the surface, then coming up and out of the water, is a marvellous image of this transition. The old life is the one that goes down into the water, a life characterised by the self-centredness we call sin; as we break the surface of the water, so we break into new life. Rising up from the water is a deliberate likeness of Jesus rising from death, freed from the sin and evil which tried to ensnare him. In baptism we are reassured of the forgiveness of sins, once and for all. Baptism also signifies our union with Christ. In many ways baptism is a sign of what has already happened, and a place from which our journey continues.

Water has its own significance. It is life-giving, of course, but in baptism it is its cleansing power which is paramount. The old life, or life without faith, is one which seems dirty, with a staining which affects all we do. But the new life, of faith, of trust, is one which is clean, bright and full of the light of God. The service puts it this way: 'By water and the Holy Spirit, God claims us as his own, washes us from sin, and sets us free from the power of death' (Common Order, p. 99).

But fundamentally, baptism is a sign of God's love. The church has long understood it as a sacrament – a sign in visible things of God's forgiving grace. When we are baptised, 'the love of God is offered to each one of us' (Common Order, p. 99). We are not baptised because we have earned God's love: it is because God loves us, a love shown in baptism, that we respond to by trusting him. For the adult believer, choosing to be baptised is an acceptance of this love, and a commitment to serve the Lord in our lives.

Of course we are free, even beyond baptism, to choose again to live in selfish ways, to turn away from others, to lose our trust in God. God's love never compels us, but always invites us to follow. As the service says, 'we are called to accept that love with the openness and trust of a child.' And the congregation prays that the one who is baptised 'may remain for ever in the number of your faithful children.'

There is then a beautiful declaration which links the faith expressed in the Apostles' Creed with the act of baptism, which claims rightly that the love of God found in Jesus Christ is for each one who is baptised as much as it is for anybody:

For you Jesus Christ came into the world:
for you he lived and showed God's love;
for you he suffered the darkness of Calvary
and cried at the last, 'It is accomplished';
for you he triumphed over death
and rose in newness of life;
for you he ascended to reign at God's right hand.
All this he did for you,
before you knew anything of it.

Then the minister pours water on the head of the one being baptised, and says simply, using his or her name, 'I baptise you in the Name of the Father, and of the Son, and of the Holy Spirit.' This form of words is common in nearly all Churches and throughout nearly all Christian history.

Immediately after that there is a blessing. The minister may say it, or sometimes the congregation sings it. The Church of Scotland has long used a setting of a blessing from the Old Testament:

The Lord bless you and keep you;
the Lord make his face to shine upon you, and be
gracious to you;
the Lord lift up his countenance upon you, and give you
peace.
(Numbers 6:24–26)

For many in the Church, singing and hearing that unhurried song, recalling as it does generations of children born and baptised, is a moving experience.

And then the service continues, and indeed so do our lives. Baptism, no more than joining the Church, is not the end-point of faith, though it may be the end of the beginning. It is a marker of our faith at a certain point in life. Occasionally, and sadly, it is the high-water mark of faith. But much more usually, faith grows beyond baptism, and the promises we make find their fulfilment in years to come, in all the places we live, the churches we belong to, and the unpredictable circumstances of life. ■

READ

Mark 1:1–11 John the Baptist baptises Jesus

Matthew 28:18–20 The disciples sent to baptise

Acts 8:26–40 Philip baptises an Ethiopian

Romans 6:1–4 Baptised into Jesus

The Church of Scotland, **By Water and the Spirit**, (Edinburgh: Saint Andrew Press, 2006)

Rowan Williams, **Being Christian**, (London: SPCK Publishing, 2014) Section 1

Tom Wright, **Simply Christian**, (London: SPCK Publishing, 2011) Section 15

THINK

1. What memories do you have of seeing the baptism of infants? Or of adults? What feelings do you recall?
2. Do you feel you are at a turning point in your life? Do you sense a call to mark such a turning point?
3. Do you believe that God's love is for you?

ACT

Why not speak with a minister about attending a baptism – or, perhaps, about being baptised yourself?

My Story
Robert McQuistan

When I reflect on what authentic Church life looks like I recall a definition of The Guild's purpose to be found on their web page.

> The Guild is about invitation, encouragement, commitment, and fellowship which lead to providing opportunities for continuing growth in Christian faith through worship, prayer and action.
>
> www.cos-guild.org.uk

I'd like to consider three aspects of Church life highlighted in this great quote.

Worship: There is a lot of debate within our Church on the subject of worship. We all have our own preferences – traditional psalms or modern instruments, hand-raising or quiet contemplation; all play a part in our Churches today.

My own experience has been in a traditional context. However, I have been heartened by the way in which local churches are beginning to explore new ideas. We need to be imaginative in the ways in which we meet together and worship – different venues, contexts and ways of engaging with individuals and the community. We are not, in other words, a *holy huddle*.

We should never forget the flexible way in which Christ conducted his own ministry – different venues, formats and ways of engaging with individuals and the community. We need, at the same time, however, to be faithful to God in prayer and worship.

Fellowship: In my own church I have always been heartened by the strong sense of close fellowship we experience; this is, of course, the experience of God's people across the nation. So, what is so special about fellowship? How does it differ from friendship?

My understanding is that a church fellowship is a community of believers who acknowledge the fact that Christian beliefs should underpin all our relationships. Fellowship is friendship informed by the virtues of forgiveness, reconciliation, mutual support, care and compassion and is inspired by the example and teachings of Christ.

Action: Throughout the New Testament, we read about faith and action working together for good. I have always found the Church to be most effective and admirable when it reaches out to the community with a supporting and compassionate hand. The care and welfare of others is central to our faith as Christians.

So, after many years of reflection, my conclusion is that healthy, productive and transformative church life is achieved by addressing the needs of our members, the community and the Word of God. Let's give it a go!

CONFIRMATION AND COMMUNION

Donald MacEwan

University Chaplain, University of St Andrews

If you have reached this far, then section by section you have explored the Church of Scotland confirmation service in the order it comes:

- professing our faith (rejecting sin, confessing need of God's forgiving grace, pledging that you glorify God and love your neighbour)
- exploring that faith in the Apostles' Creed
- baptism

What follows is confirmation, or joining the Church. It comes in a prayer and welcome. It is a prayer, because we believe it is God who confirms, God who forgives, God who invites us to share in the community of his Son Jesus Christ, God who calls us to be part of the holy catholic Church. We cannot make ourselves Christians; we cannot put ourselves into the Church: God calls, God gives, God welcomes. The candidate for confirmation kneels, and the minister lays hands on the candidate, the physical touch expressing God's love for this person, and prays:

Defend, O Lord, your servant [adding his or her name]
with your heavenly grace,
that he or she may continue yours for ever,
and daily increase in your Holy spirit
until he or she comes to your everlasting kingdom.
Amen.

It is an intriguing prayer. In beginning, 'Defend, O Lord ...' there is an acknowledgment that the Christian life is not lived in Eden. Our relationships in our family, among friends and at work; the pressures we face at the workplace; ill health in body or mind; news of natural disaster and human cruelty – all these can threaten our continuing relationship with God. And so the prayer of confirmation recognises that by ourselves we cannot maintain the faith. Our trust in God depends on God's faithfulness to us.

When the newly confirmed stand, they are welcomed by the minister:

In the name of the Lord Jesus Christ,
the King and Head of the Church,
and by the authority of this Kirk Session,
I welcome and receive you
within the fellowship of the Lord's Table
and admit you
to the full privileges of the children of God
and to the responsibilities of membership
within this congregation
of the one holy catholic and apostolic Church.
May your sharing in our life together
bring blessing to you and to us all.

The welcome is to the particular Church of Scotland congregation in question. (The *Kirk Session* is the name for the group of elders, led by the minister, which oversees the spiritual – and sometimes the practical – life of the congregation.) But it is also a welcome to the Church as a whole. Although there are so many different branches of the Church, the minister expresses a welcome into God's Church, into the body of his Son Jesus Christ, where his unity matters much more than our differences.

There are three aspects of this welcome. The last is 'the responsibilities of membership' which we will explore in the next section. The second is 'the full privileges of the children of God', a curious and slightly old-fashioned phrase. It serves to reassure the newly confirmed that they are as much a part of the Church as anybody, that theirs is no second-class membership, that there is no deeper level of membership to which they must aspire. God's forgiving grace is for them as much as for anybody – this echoes those words said to those about to be baptised, 'For you Jesus Christ came into the world ...'

But let us explore the first aspect of the welcome a little more deeply: 'I welcome and receive you within the fellowship of the Lord's Table.' This makes explicit the link between joining the Church and receiving communion, for the Lord's Table refers to the common meal of bread and wine.

Communion

When I joined the Church of Scotland, I had never been to a communion service there before. It was a mysterious affair, to which children were not invited and which was only for members. My parents' communion cards, brought by our elder some days before, would sit on the hall shelf until the morning of the service, which took place three times a year. It was only when I joined the Church that I was allowed to receive communion. This understanding is reflected in the full title of the service for joining the Church – *Order for the Public Profession of Faith, Confirmation, and Admission to the Lord's Supper.*

Today the situation is less rigid. Communion is generally celebrated more often. Many congregations of the Church of Scotland allow children to receive communion, and often a communion service will begin with an invitation to all baptised Christians to feel free to receive, whether or not confirmed. There is, in general, less solemnity than before – which is true of many other aspects of Church life.

The origins of the Lord's Supper, or Communion (or the Eucharist as it is also known) are in the Last Supper, the Passover meal Jesus shared with his disciples the night of his arrest, the night before he died. Jesus himself associates bread with his body and wine with his blood. Body and blood together convey the sense of a whole life broken and poured out for the world, sealed finally and completely in his death on the cross.

The early Church repeated this meal, as a memorial of Jesus, as thanksgiving for his self-giving love found in his life and death, as a celebration of his presence with us, raised from the dead, alive with us by his Spirit, and as nourishment for our Christian life and faith. In time, it became known as a sacrament, a sign in visible form of the invisible forgiving grace of Christ. Exactly how Christ is present in communion has been one point on which Churches have disagreed down the centuries, and the sacrament of communion remains divisive due to the differing understandings in the Church over who may receive from whom.

For some Christians, especially Roman Catholic, Orthodox and many Anglican, receiving communion is the central act of their faith, the principal way in which God's grace is received. They may receive communion weekly or even daily, if possible. For others, communion is considered to be so special a sign of God's grace that it is not received in an everyday manner but much less often, perhaps once or twice a year, and following a period of preparation. But for all, it allows for a profound experience and assurance of the truth of Jesus' words: 'I am the bread of life. Whoever comes to me will never be hungry, and whoever believes in me will never be thirsty.' (John 6:35) ∎

> Jesus associates bread with his body and wine with his blood.

READ

Luke 22:14–23 The last supper

Luke 24:13–35 The risen Jesus recognised in the breaking of bread

1 Corinthians 11:23–26 Paul's narrative of the last supper

Stephen Cottrell *et al.*, **Pilgrim: the Eucharist**, (London: Church House Publishing, 2014)

D. M. Baillie, **The Theology of the Sacraments**, (London: Charles Scribner's Sons, 1957) Section 2

Dave Tomlinson, **How to be a Bad Christian ... And a Better Human Being**, (London: Hodder & Stroughton, 2012) Section 14

Rowan Williams, **Being Christian**, (London: SPCK Publishing, 2014) Section 3

THINK

1. What prayer would you make in being confirmed? Would it start, 'Defend me, O Lord, from ...'?

2. Are you ready to join the church?

3. 'The early church repeated this meal:

   • as a memorial of Jesus,

   • as thanksgiving for his self-giving love found in his life and death,

   • as a celebration of his presence with us, raised from the dead, alive with us by his Spirit, and

   • as nourishment for our Christian life and faith.'

Which of these aspects of communion seems significant to you?

ACT

Why not attend a communion service at your local church?

WHAT ABOUT OTHER CHURCHES?

Matthew Ross
General Secretary, Action of Churches Together in Scotland

In John 17:21, Jesus prayed that his followers 'may all be one'. Following the prayer of Jesus, the Church of Scotland takes Christian unity seriously.

The Church of Scotland is a national Church, but this should not be seen as a position of superiority over other denominations. The calling to be a national Church means a responsibility towards all parts of the country – including the very rural and remote. Delivering this objective can include co-operation with other Churches.

The opening words of the Articles Declaratory of the Church of Scotland (which act like guiding principles) state: 'The Church of Scotland is part of the Holy Catholic or Universal Church ...' In speaking of 'other' Churches, the unity of the Church transcends denominations. We believe that Christ is the King and Head of the Church.

Unity and uniformity are not the same thing. Two millennia of Christian history have resulted in differing traditions, cultures and theological interpretations. The first major split in the Church came in 1054, with the East–West Schism resulting in the division of Eastern

> **In working together, the churches may also recognise their common faith in Christ and together work to realise Christ's prayer for unity.**

Orthodoxy from Roman Catholicism. The next major split came in the sixteenth century, with the Reformation in central Europe subsequently spreading to other lands. The Scottish Reformation, inspired by John Knox, took place in 1560, with a Presbyterian system of church government slowly being consolidated between the 1580s and 1690s.

Scotland's history has been marked by theological disagreement, occasionally violent, including the executions of the Protestant Reformers Patrick Hamilton (in 1528) and George Wishart (in

1546) and – following the Reformation in 1560 – of the Jesuit Priest John Ogilvie (in 1615). As recently as 1923 the Church of Scotland published a report entitled 'The Menace of the Irish Race to our Scottish Nationality' – a virulently anti-Roman Catholic document. Such divisive views have inevitably had major social consequences, especially for dissenters from the majority.

Much has changed in recent decades. The Church of Scotland has acknowledged its past contributions to division – including formally dissociating itself (in 1986) from the anti-Papal sections of the 1647 Westminster Confession of Faith. The General Assembly also formally repudiated the 'Menace of the Irish Race' report (in 2002). The Church of Scotland has also worked to address the continuing legacy of sectarianism and the resulting social divisions, and there now exists a flourishing Joint Commission on Doctrine of the Church of Scotland and the Roman Catholic Church in Scotland.

The twentieth century saw considerable moves towards better ecumenical relations, both nationally and internationally. Ecumenism, based on the Greek word for 'the whole inhabited earth', is essentially a movement of Churches that believe that their divisions weaken the witness they are called to give as the one Church of Jesus Christ to God's loving purpose of reconciliation, wholeness, peace and justice for the whole of creation in which the relations within the human community, and between the human community and the environment, are of critical importance. The 1910 Edinburgh Missionary Conference is often regarded as the birth of the global ecumenical movement.

The Church of Scotland was a founder member of the World Council of Churches in 1948. The Church of Scotland is a member of the Brussels-based Conference of European Churches (CEC) – with Reformed, Lutheran, Orthodox, Anglican and Old Catholic member Churches. In 1973, the signing of the Leuenberg Agreement facilitated mutual recognition internationally between Lutheran and Reformed churches (including the Church of Scotland).

In 1990, the Church of Scotland and the Roman Catholic Church became founder members of both Churches Together in Britain & Ireland (CTBI) and Action of Churches Together in Scotland (ACTS). The other member Churches of ACTS are the Congregational Federation, Methodist Church, Religious Society of Friends (Quakers), Salvation Army, Scottish Episcopal Church, United Free Church of Scotland and United Reformed Church. ACTS aims to bring Christians of different traditions in Scotland closer to one another in their shared faith in Jesus Christ by meeting, praying, learning, reflecting and acting together on matters of common concern.

An important ecumenical initiative in the late twentieth century was the opening of Scottish Churches House in 1960. The House, based in Dunblane, played a key role in allowing Christians of differing denominations to gather and share ideas. Although the House closed in 2011, the lasting change in attitudes towards ecumenical relations during these decades has created a very positive legacy.

In the late twentieth century, the Scottish Churches Initiative for Union (SCIFU) was an attempt to unite the Church of Scotland, Scottish Episcopal Church, Methodist Church (in Scotland) and the United Reformed Church (in Scotland). In 2003, the Church of Scotland decided to withdraw from the SCIFU negotiations, but nevertheless cordial relations continue between all four denominations – both under the auspices of ACTS and through local initiatives.

Several Church of Scotland congregations are part of 'Local Ecumenical Partnerships'. These congregations are in full membership of more than one denomination – for example Morningside United Church in Edinburgh is part of both the Church of Scotland and the United Reformed Church. Many of the Church of Scotland's congregations in continental Europe are also full members of local denominations, for example St Andrew's Church in Brussels is part of the Church of Scotland and the United Protestant Church of Belgium.

Local ecumenical 'Churches Together' groups exist in many Scottish towns and cities, for example in Glasgow, Perth, Bishopbriggs and Banff. Informal relations at a grassroots levels are of crucial importance in living out Jesus' prayer of unity in John 17:21.

Many church denominations in Europe – including Scotland – are facing acute challenges from declining membership and increasing secularism in society. This raises the need for increasing co-operation for effective mission and outreach. In working together, the churches may also recognise their common faith in Christ and together work to realise Christ's prayer for unity. ■

READ

Romans 14 Do not pass judgement on one another

Church of Scotland website (pages on ecumenism): **www.churchofscotland.org.uk/connect/ecumenism**

Action of Churches Together in Scotland: **www.acts-scotland.org**

Churches Together in Britain & Ireland: **www.ctbi.org.uk**

Conference of European Churches: **www.ceceurope.org**

World Council of Churches: **www.oikoumene.org**

THINK

1. Reflect on the significance of Jesus' prayer in John 17:20-23; how does this change our perception towards the need for Christian unity at a local, national or international level?

2. How could your congregation cooperate ecumenically within your local area?

3. How can sharing resources (such as equipment, buildings, holiday clubs, etc.) free up other resources for mission?

ACT

Why not attend a worship meeting at another church, and introduce yourself?

MEMBERSHIP PROMISES: WORSHIP, BIBLE AND PRAYER

Donald MacEwan
University Chaplain, University of St Andrews

O nly now are the newly-confirmed asked to make promises. They matter but they are not a pre-condition of joining the church. Rather, the making of these promises follows the act of faith. They are a response to God's love, not the key that would unlock his grace. They give a strong hint as to what is important in Christian living, and in belonging to the church. But they cannot cover all the ground: they are like lamps which illuminate a stretch of the road but leave other parts barely lit. In the same way, there are large parts of life in which there is no clear rule from the Christian faith, or from the confirmation service. Instead we have to develop our character as Christians. Although it may be slightly simplistic to follow the wristband's prompt/ question of WWJD – *What would Jesus do?* – the principle of enquiring after God's will is sound.

There are two sets of promises approved by the Church of Scotland. Let's look at both. They are quite similar but are expressed in different kinds of language. First we will look at the set of promises that are written in more traditional language and these follow over the next two sections. Then, on page 63, we'll look at the less traditional set.

we have to develop our character as Christians.

Worship

In the more traditional set, the first question is about worship:

Do you promise to join regularly
with your fellow Christians
in worship on the Lord's Day?

Worship can be among the most beautiful, moving, satisfying experiences of life. It can also be a dispiriting, boring or even upsetting event. Often it is somewhere in the middle – not quite a mountain-top experience but offering something which the rest of life does not contain. Its contents have been fairly constant over the centuries and across the Churches – prayer, readings from the Bible, hymns and music, a sermon and silence, communion and blessing. But every element is open to boundless variety – as is the order itself.

In my life I have worshipped in a Japanese Pentecostal church, Roman Catholic churches in Rome, Methodist churches in Ohio, an Anglican church in Uganda, and Orthodox churches from Belarus to St Andrews. All have unique styles, emphases, languages and feel – but all worship. Even the Church of Scotland has a broad range of worship patterns from praise bands through traditional hymns to gowned choirs singing Renaissance anthems in Latin. Preaching may be anything from a drama sketch to a 40-minute exposition of the Bible passage. Prayer may be formal with the same set words weekly in a set order, or a much more improvised outpouring from the heart of the person praying.

But despite these differences there is always something in common and unique to worship. It is a time and space in which we acknowledge that we are not in charge, that ours is not the last word, that our lives are bound by God. Worship takes place when we say, sing, think and feel that God is our creator, that God is our rescuer and that God is present with us. Worship is the expression of our thankfulness for this, our dependence on his grace, and our inability to solve the world's problems by our strength alone. Worship is the inspiration to us to take responsibility for the world, to love our neighbour – not because of our independent human capability, but because of the task entrusted to us by one whose creative love never gives up caring for people who are hurting. Worship is a time and space of trust. It is experiencing what we believe.

It is possible to be a Christian and worship infrequently, but that is hard. I remember one fine witty woman in a parish I served in who used to say, 'I wish I was a good enough Christian not to need to go to church.' Joining regularly with our fellow Christians on Sunday (or other times of worship) builds faith and trust, knowledge and interest, community and love.

The Bible

*Do you promise
to be faithful in reading the Bible
and in prayer?*

In some ways reading has never been so popular. We read constantly, a snatch of a website here, a quick email there, a brief column in a magazine. In restaurants, couples sit opposite each other, but spend the time between courses reading – scrolling through texts and emails, checking the internet on their phones. But in other ways, reading is becoming a rare ability. Reading for a while, reading a section of a novel, or even the whole book takes a power of concentration which we seem to be losing. Yet the Christian faith would not exist without a book, one which people have read. That book is the Bible.

Here's the quickest of potted histories of the Bible. It was written mainly in Hebrew and Greek in something a bit over a thousand years. The Hebrew books, which Christians call the Old Testament, were written by the people of Israel, worshippers of the one God. There are books of history and law, books of prophecy and wisdom, laments of despair and songs of praise to God. It tells the story of creation, of God's call to a people to be *God's* people, of their becoming a kingdom, of the ways this creation and kingdom go wrong, and of their hope for rescue.

The Greek books, which Christians call the New Testament, were written later by worshippers of the one God and who believed Jesus to be the Messiah, the Son of God. It tells the story of Jesus' birth, life, death and resurrection, of the first Christians, the coming of the Holy Spirit and the expansion of the Church.

Together, this Bible tells the story of God's creation, his interaction with his people, his persistent, vulnerable love, found unsurpassably in Jesus, his mission to save, his presence and his promise. The Apostles' Creed is a re-telling, in a very abbreviated form, of some of the central features of the Bible's sprawling mix of story, poetry, law, theology and vision.

But the Bible is more than a source-book for the faith into which we are enquiring. God speaks through it. When we read the Bible, it becomes alive. It can convey what God is saying to us. It becomes the word of God. And so if Christians want to hear the voice of God, and know what God is saying to them, how he is guiding them, what challenges he is making of them, they read the Bible.

Christians believe in the authority of the Bible. It is, for members of the Church of Scotland, 'the supreme rule of life and faith'. But different Christians don't always interpret the scriptures in exactly the same way. Different readers give different weight to certain sections and emphases. Some stress the humanity of its writers, and the way in which understanding of God grows or even changes through the Bible. Others tend to see the scriptures as the true revelation of God in every verse, not one of which verses can be laid aside as not applicable to us today. Furthermore, different readers bring a different mix of other influences to bear when reading the Bible – our reason, modern knowledge, our experience and the traditions of the church. But regardless of the different interpretations we may hold, all Christians believe scripture to be authoritative, for all believe that God speaks through it.

This happens in church, of course, where we hear the Bible, and may read it on a screen or in a copy in front of us. But Christians also read the Bible in small groups and at home, alone, or on the bus, or listen to it in the car. And when they do that, and if they ask God to speak to them when they read, it often happens. They may sense a particular word or phrase or sentence or episode has relevance to their life. They may feel that a story offers parallels to their own story. They may feel that an instruction shows an area of their life which is wrong. They may be comforted by a promise, excited by an argument, inspired by an image. They may realise that God is speaking through the Bible to their own society.

You could start at Genesis and keep going till the last section of Revelation. I did that, from the age of 17, though my grand plan to read the Bible in a year somehow took closer to four. But many people read a little bit each day, with the help of notes, questions and prayers provided in Bible-reading notes in print or online. There are plenty of good modern translations, as well as beautiful, older ones. You can download it to whatever device you use – which may make you less inhibited when on the bus.

 all Christians believe scripture to be authoritative, for all believe that God speaks through it.

Prayer

Prayer, like worship, acknowledges that we are not in charge of ourselves. It is a placing of our thoughts, our worries, our hopes, our gladness and our regret with God, a trusting him with ourselves. It can take the form of words, in spoken prayers or prayers said inside our heads. It can follow a set pattern, laid down for the day in a book or on a website. Or it can flow freely from the concerns of our heart. We could draw up a list of people and situations to pray for each day, or wait to see what issues or people rise to the surface of our thoughts. Some people pray upon rising from bed, putting the day into God's hands. Others pray last thing at night, looking back, giving thanks, giving the day back to God. Others pepper the day with prayer, perhaps just a *Thanks* or *Sorry* or *Help!* Many find praying with others a significant experience – in church services or Bible study groups.

But not all prayer is words. Lighting a candle, letting the light burn, is a prayer which many do in churches and elsewhere. Listening to the sounds around us, or our own breathing or our own body, could be prayer. Meditating on a story or a line from scripture, staying with a thought or image which emerges could be prayer. Walking in woods, or on a beach, or by a river could be prayer. How so? Anything which helps us be with *our self*, and sense *our self* in relation to God can be prayer.

Some think it strange to pray – doesn't God know everything anyway? Yes, perhaps he does, but as a loving presence, unceasingly and precariously offering himself to the world, this love does not coerce. It invites. And so our prayer is a response, in faith and love, to his invitation to communicate, to share, to be part of his people.

Another problem people have with prayer is whether or not it works. Scientists have examined whether praying for people recovering from surgery improves their chances of survival – and the evidence seems to point to prayer having no effect. So why pray for things to change? Let me suggest why it is still a good thing to do. First, prayer is not magic: it is not a spell which God is obliged to make come true. God loves the world in freedom: prayer to God does ask God to act, but cannot manipulate him. Further, it may be that what we ask for is not the will of God. 'For we know only in part ... For now we see in a mirror, dimly' (1 Corinthians 13:9, 12). God, by contrast, sees the whole picture so that our view compared to his is like a single brushstroke on a vast canvas. This does not necessarily imply that everything that happens is God's will. But, perhaps more importantly, prayer may well coincide with reality taking a different course. Many Christians experience prayer as leading to 'coincidences' which cease to occur when they cease to pray.

Not all prayers are answered; and certainly not all are answered as we wish. There are Christians in whom a deep disappointment grows, like a jagged, dirty, grey pearl in the oyster, as an answer to prayer increasingly seems unlikely. It could be for love, or for a child, or for freedom from depression, or for a child's success, or for release from pain. 'Why doesn't he answer?' The truth is: I don't know. There is a mystery in suffering which faith does not always diminish. Unanswered prayer can often be one of the hardest aspects of the Christian experience. But faith does say: *we face this suffering with God, we face it in hope, and we continue to pray. As God's love does not give up, so neither do we.* ■

READ

Psalm 1:1–3 Delight in the Law of the Lord

2 Timothy 3:16 All scripture ...

Luke 10:38–42 Mary and Martha

Luke 11:1–13 Lord's Prayer, and more

Luke 5:16 Jesus withdraws to pray by himself

Rowan Williams, **Being Christian**, (London: SPCK Publishing, 2014) Sections 2 and 4

Tom Wright, **Simply Christian**, (London: SPCK Publishing, 2011) Sections 11–14

Philip Yancey, **Prayer: does it make any difference?** (London: Hodder and Stroughton, 2008)

Pray Now Group, **Living Stones**, (Edinburgh: Saint Andrew Press, 2015)

THINK

1. Think of a time of worship which was significant for you. What made it so?

2. How would you fulfil the promise to be faithful in reading the Bible?

3. How would you fulfil the promise to be faithful in prayer?

ACT

Why not use a prayer resource such as *Living Stones* (www.standrewpress.com) and try the prayers and meditations?

SECULARISM AND FAITH

David Fergusson
Professor of Divinity and Principal of New College, University of Edinburgh

As we approach this topic it is helpful to reflect upon a particular word: 'saeculum'. This Latin word means 'world' and formerly referred to the domain outside the Church. Although distinguished from the ecclesiastical (Church) sphere, the secular was neither detached from it nor in opposition to it. In the Middle Ages, for example, monks could be religious or secular in relation to their particular sphere of service. When they left the monastery to serve God in the wider world, they became secularised. The Reformation in Scotland was also a movement which sought to align the religious and the secular in a shared partnership under the rule of God.

Since about the seventeenth century, however, the 'secular' has taken on new meanings which contrast it with the scope and influence of the Church. A central element of western democracy is the relative neutrality of the state and the public sphere in relation to the authority of the Church. This means, for example, that one can vote, hold public office, enter the professions and be entitled to education, health care and other services irrespective of one's faith

> **The state is not entitled to privilege the members of one religious party or to disadvantage those of another ...**

commitment. The state is not entitled to privilege the members of one religious party or to disadvantage those of another. In this respect, the equality of all citizens is closely associated with state neutrality and the establishment of a secular sphere in which different religious bodies can function peacefully alongside each other.

This ideal of secularism has been espoused by defenders of liberal democracy, particularly in the West, but also in countries like Turkey and India, though there are wide variations in expression even in Europe. We find different models which range from those which attempt a strict exclusion of religion from the secular – perhaps France might be the best example here – to others such as the UK which aim to show impartiality in their treatment of different religious groups. The best-known example of secularism considered as state neutrality is in the United States of America where the First Amendment to the Constitution prohibits the establishment of any single religious body. This has sometimes been referred to as 'the high wall of separation' (Thomas Jefferson) between Church and State, though Christianity retains a strong hold on American culture today.

In some parts of Europe, secularism appears to be compatible with the establishment or recognition of national Churches, the levying of Church taxes, and the provision of publicly funded faith schools. Nevertheless, the general trend in most societies is towards the equal treatment of religious groups, and, where special arrangements continue to hold, these are justified as promoting the common good while not infringing upon the rights of citizens. This is secularism considered as a political phenomenon and it can be held alongside a strong faith commitment. In this way, many Christians could consistently be secularists in terms of the society that they seek to promote for their fellow citizens.

We can also distinguish secularism as an ideology, which is more threatening to faith. It is a way of explaining the world, society and human persons in terms that do not require any reference to God or the transcendent. Several philosophies that emerged in the eighteenth century provide a good example of such secularism, including that of David Hume (1711–1776), the leading figure of the Scottish Enlightenment. Secularism in this stronger sense is incompatible with religious explanation. It is directly in competition with faith and seeks to displace it by a natural or secular account of moral values and public institutions. In this stronger ideological sense, it is often combined with secularism in the aforementioned political sense. Historically, it coincides with the emergence of fields of enquiry which became independent of the control and influence of the Churches, e.g. the natural sciences and economics.

This form of secularism often results in arguments for the comprehensive exclusion of religion from the public sphere. For example, it is claimed that the public advocacy of religious principles is intolerant, divisive and destructive of a multi-cultural society. Therefore ideological secularism will typically offer a strong reading of state neutrality, not so much as impartiality but as the non-intrusion of religion into public life. Several exponents of the new atheism are secularists in this double sense; they wish to replace a religious account of the world with a secular one, while also insisting on political grounds that religion belongs to a private life-style choice and should not intrude in public debates or social organisation. So it is argued, often quite vehemently, that legislation on abortion, assisted dying or genetic engineering should not be shaped in any way by distinctively religious considerations. This, of course, raises the problem of which moral sentiments are to be admitted into public discourse and who is to be their arbiter.

A recent distinction between 'programmatic' and 'procedural' secularism has been introduced by Rowan Williams and might help us to think through these issues. This corresponds to our two senses of secularism:

- a programmatic secularism is the strong secularism which is committed ideologically to secular principles and politically to the removal of religion from public life

- a procedural secularism, by contrast, aims to provide a relatively neutral public space in which different groups can exchange ideas, participate actively and argue with civility on the basis of their deepest convictions.

When you consider the increasingly diverse religious complexion of our society, including large numbers who identify as belonging to no religion, there is an obvious need to promote a healthy procedural secularism without capitulating to the programmatic secularism – which is the ideological position of only a small minority. A procedural secularism can be combined with a commitment to a multi-faith and pluralist society. ■

READ

Jonathan Chaplin, **Talking God: the legitimacy of religious public reasoning**, (London: Theos, 2008): **http://www.theosthinktank.co.uk/files/files/Reports/TalkingGod1.pdf**

Rowan Williams, **Faith in the Public Square**, (London: Bloomsbury, 2012)

THINK

1. What examples from recent public life illustrate secular demands to exclude religious expression?

2. In what ways can faith-based positions still be effectively communicated in our world?

3. What benefits has secularism produced and how might these best be preserved?

ACT

Read Romans 12–13 and consider how Paul's teaching might best be applied today in a multi-cultural society.

MEMBERSHIP: TIME AND TALENTS

Donald MacEwan
University Chaplain, University of St Andrews

The second two promises of membership take a slightly more practical, outward-looking turn.

Do you promise to give a fitting proportion of your time, talents and money for the Church's work in the world?

Time

Cash-rich time-poor. We work long hours today. Much of our leisure time is spent doing things that other people used to do as part of their work – so we spend our evenings and weekends on DIY, or booking holidays, or online banking. Our children demand our presence; and so does housework. Time on our mobile phones and social media cuts into everything else.

But time is God's gift. As creator of heaven and earth, God gives time. As with all God's gifts, we are called to receive it humbly, and use it wisely as good stewards. And so we should not use time only for our individual pursuits, and shield our time from the commitments of faith. Rather, we should be open to giving time to the church, as part of our response to God's grace, in fitting proportion.

some Christians are called to a particular form of work.

Talents

What then should we do with this time? That leads to the next element of our commitment: talents. These again are the gift of God, and so we offer our talents for the work of the Church as part of our grateful response to God's love. The talents we give relate to the huge variety of life in the Church: from joining the choir, to playing football at an outreach event. Or you could be a gifted listener, and so join a pastoral care team; or if a talented teacher, help with the Sunday School; or if good with numbers, part of the finance committee; or if you have a steady hand and a head for heights, you might redecorate the church hall. In fact, your church will have a unique set of activities, because it may well have developed these things around the gifts of the people.

For some people, a fitting proportion of their time and talents involves responding to a further call. The Church of Scotland ordains elders. These are people whom the local church identifies as having the faith, commitment and gifts to lead the congregation as members of the Kirk Session, and to serve the people.

Others feel a call to ordained ministry. You may be reading this and have a sense that you are called to a life of ministry. You may be hesitant, especially if this is early days for your faith. That's all right. A call to ministry requires exploring, rather than instant acceptance or dismissal. Tell someone about this sense of calling, perhaps your minister, read further about ministry, and take the time to discern whether this could be God's call for you. Visit the Church of Scotland website for more information.

Money

The call to Christian living is not a partial thing: it involves the whole of life, including money. Money too is a gift from God. All our goods, all our possessions, all that exists is part of God's creation. And so we give a fitting proportion of our money to the church as part of our thanksgiving to God for what he has done for us, in creation, in rescue, in presence.

How much is a fitting proportion? A traditional answer was a tithe, often a tenth of our income. Some people do follow that. More recently, the Church of Scotland has encouraged *sacrificial giving*, which is giving not merely what we can spare from the loose change of our lives, but serious giving which may have a knock-on effect on some of our other choices. More information on giving, and on where the money which we give to the church goes, can be found from the Stewardship team on the Church of Scotland website.

Loyalty and service

The final promise is this:

Do you promise,
depending on the grace of God,
to profess publicly your loyalty to Jesus Christ,
to serve him in your daily work,
and to walk in his ways all the days of your life?

Finally, then, we commit to all this by 'depending on the grace of God.' Fulfilling the other promises may implicitly depend on God's grace, his forgiving love, his strength and inspiration. But it is made explicit here: this is not easy. This is a promise to be a Christian of integrity beyond the church – in our families, among our friends, at work and in society.

Public loyalty

Professing publicly your loyalty to Jesus Christ initially seems to be about speaking about our faith with others. The principle is simple: the more we explore the Christian faith, the more we believe in God, the more we follow Jesus Christ, the more we want others to share this exploration, this faith, this experience – this is known as witnessing. For example, when a conversation takes a turn towards deeper subjects, of life, death, purpose, right and wrong, justice and hope, Christians may share the reality of their own belief and commitment. It takes courage, particularly in settings where there is a general ridicule of all things religious. But the grace of God gives such courage.

There is a further aspect to public profession of loyalty to Jesus Christ, and that is how we live. Indeed, what we do and how we are seen may be more significant in our witnessing than what we say. We say we follow Jesus, but do we live as he did? Here are some things that following Jesus means: compassion, self-sacrifice, honesty, generosity, peace-making, humility, commitment to the poor. And in a story Jesus told about caring for others, it is in caring for the neediest of the needy that Jesus himself is encountered (see Matthew 25:31–40).

Daily work

Serving Jesus in our daily work has a twofold aspect. First, it provides a context for that public profession we've just been looking at. The workplace – or wherever we work, from the kitchen to the internet – is the context for much of our lives, and for the integrity we are called on to have. That may involve questioning how to live out our Christian faith in a workplace where there are difficult moral issues. What we're called to do is to develop our character as Christians, and expect that from such character wisdom will emerge to help us face the particular issues we face at work.

The second aspect is the work itself. As we saw earlier, some Christians are called to a particular form of work, often ministry, sometimes a different job. But far more do work which is not specifically Christian. Yet they are still called – not to Christian work, but to be a Christian in their work. And this is part of our Christian response to God too.

Walking in Jesus' ways

The final line of this last promise when being confirmed is one which explicitly looks forward to the rest of life. Walking in the ways of Jesus Christ all the days of our life is a commitment, akin to marriage, regardless of the circumstances which follow, the surprises and routines, the setbacks and joys. Ask any Christian who has followed Jesus for many years, and they will tell you it is not always a smooth ride. There are bumps, swerves and sometimes breakdowns. Our faith can deepen, but so can our doubts. We can find worship enormously satisfying but then for a while it seems stale and irrelevant. Our commitment to God's world can be immensely fulfilling, such as serving in a food bank, but then it suddenly seems a futile gesture given the relentlessness of suffering. We find ourselves questioning our once-strong moral convictions. We can feel let down by Christian family, friends and ministers, and hurt by the church's actions, pronouncements and silences. We can lose our faith, temporarily or completely.

But then what did we expect? Jesus' life, of love, honesty, truth and commitment led to his execution by forces deeply frightened by his influence. He defeated death in rising to life, but the world still awaits the full completion of this victory. Until then, the world is subject to sorrow, suffering and evil. We will not walk faultlessly, and we will not walk on smooth paths. But we promise, nonetheless, to walk. The most moving encounters I have had with Christians have been with those who are still walking in Jesus' ways – still loving, still praying, still thinking, still working for the Church – despite lives which have known grief, rejection and pain. They have probably forgotten the words of the promises they made when joining the Church. But the promises are fulfilled daily in their lives. ∎

READ

Mark 8:34–37 The cost of following Jesus

1 Corinthians 12 Spiritual gifts

Matthew 10:16–20 Spirit will speak through us

Hebrews 12:1–2 Running the race, looking to Jesus

Gary Badcock, **The Way of Life**, (Grand Rapids: Eerdmans, 1998)

Raymond L. Hilgert, Philip H. Lochhaas and James L. Truesdell, **Christian Ethics in the Workplace**, (Missouri: Concordia Publishing House, 2001)

Dietrich Bonhoeffer, **The Cost of Discipleship**, (London: SCM Press, 1959)

THINK

1. What is a fitting proportion of time, talents and money for you?
2. What are the contexts where you'll be called on to profess publicly your loyalty to Jesus Christ?
3. What are you looking forward to in faith? What fills you with worry?

ACT

Visit the Church of Scotland Stewardship page to discover how to make the most of your talents and gifts within the Church.

http://www.churchofscotland.org.uk/resources/subjects/national_stewardship_programmes

VOCATION AND CALLING

Neil Glover
Convener of Ministries Council, Church of Scotland

Why speak of the Apostles' Creed and vocation when the creed itself avoids such talk? Strikingly it contains nothing obvious on questions of where we should live, how we should conduct our friendship, or to what career we should give ourselves. Indeed this is a creed short of any form of instruction: it does not even tell us to love kindly, walk humbly, witness boldly or campaign persistently.

It may be that this is because such questions matter little – that all the Creed requires is that we speak it with as much confidence as we can muster and God will be satisfied. As if these are words under which we must tick the box marked 'I agree' and move on to the other questions of our lives.

Or perhaps there is something else going on here? Perhaps the silence about vocation is really posing us some kind of question. Now that much has been said of God (the creator Father; the virgin-born, crucified, dead, buried, and raised Son; the Holy Spirit) and a little of humanity (the saints, the Church, the sins that are forgiven, the body that will be resurrected), what now of the last word, what now of 'life', specifically your life, in particular, what of your eternal life? Though phrased as statements, the Creed is really a question: 'How now will you live in this God-drenched universe?'

the Creed is really a question: How now will you live in this God-drenched universe?

The scriptures move frequently from talk about God to questions about life. The Genesis creation account begins with 'In the beginning God' and ends with humanity's call to fruitful multiplying and stewardship of the earth. When Jesus starts announcing the nearness of God, he immediately starts calling people to be disciples. The Gospel of John opens with 'In the beginning was the Word ... the Word became flesh' and closes with the disciples being called to life of service. Ephesians 4 and its majestic 'one Lord, one faith, one baptism, one God and Father of all, who is above all and through all and in all' is laced with the language of call – 'I therefore, the prisoner in the Lord, beg you to lead a life worthy of the calling to which you have been called', 'just as you were called to the one hope of your calling'.

When the Bible reaches into its richest vocabulary to speak of God, it is not long before it is calling us to live a different sort of life. In a universe of a God who does remarkable things, it seems that we are similarly called to do remarkable things, almost in imitation, almost that we might become part of the work of this remarkable God.

Parker Palmer, who has written some of our finest recent texts on call and vocation, traces this logic in the other direction. He writes that the deepest vocational question is not 'What ought I to do with my life?' but the far more demanding 'Who am I? What is my nature?', and that the question 'Who am I?' leads to the even more demanding question 'Whose am I?' It seems that God-talk leads to questions of life, and life-talk leads to questions of God.

So, what can we say of life in this universe which was made by this God? If this is not a God of casual accidents but a God who makes things good; and if God made me, then somehow I am called to display that goodness in the world by being who I was created to be, and doing what I was created to do. I am not simply a collection of atoms, however pleasingly arranged. God has made me for something more – something that has a purpose, an intention, a meaning.

And if this God has called me to life in this world, then this life is for God. My life cannot be about my pleasures, my rank, my conquests and acquisitions; rather it must be a life which is offered for God. It is to be given up and risked; it is to be let go of, in order that it may be found. The paradox is that risking all is our safest bet.

And this is to be done without panic. Calling is not something at which we only get one shot, something which must be found by our twenty-fifth birthday, anxiously wondered if we have missed when we are 40 and retired from when we are 65. Rather, it is something for babies (possibly even the unborn if John's antenatal leaping in Luke 1:41 sets a precedent) and pensioners (Sarah getting pregnant in her 90s springs to mind from the book of Genesis) and even beyond. Being called into eternal life is to start to think about how we live everyday with purpose.

And such calling is not only about general talk of fulfilling our baptism, loving our neighbours and running the race set before us. Amongst many other specifics, it is also about our careers. Barbara Brown Taylor has reminded us that the Church is a gathering of priests with many different altars.

Christians are called to serve in a variety of ministries – from the surgeon in the operating theatre helping to serve and heal God's creation, to the writer or engineer taking part in stewardship.

One career to which some may be called is that of parish ministry. John Bell has said that there are three requirements for such a task: love of God, love of people and love of words. The call is to help lead the Church in its worship, its discipling, its evangelism and its mission. The call to such ministry may be your call, and, if it is, then it will come as a call from the creative, redemptive, indwelling God, whose call always comes as something which is both unavoidably obvious and a total surprise. ∎

READ

Parker J. Palmer, **Let Your Life Speak: listening for the voice of vocation**, (San Francisco: Jossey-Bass, 2000) pp. 15–17

Barbara Brown Taylor, **The Preaching Life: living out your vocation**, (London: Canterbury Press, 2013) p. 37

THINK

1. What do you feel called to do?

2. How could you glorify God in your vocation, whatever role you have been placed in?

3. Do you think that you could be called to ministry?

ACT

Why not pray for guidance in living authentically as who you were created to be, and doing what you were created to do?

Why not look at **www.churchofscotland.org. uk/tomorrowscalling**

TOMORROW'S CALLING

churchofscotland.org.uk/tomorrowscalling

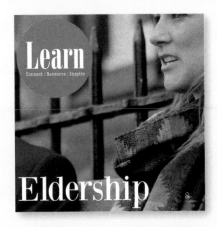

My Story **Abi Ngunga**

I was born and raised in the Democratic Republic of Congo before moving to Scotland in 2005. My life took a significant turn after accepting the Lord Jesus Christ and becoming a Christian in 1985. Since then, the rest of my life can be summed up in the words of Rufus Henry McDaniel's (1850–1940) song:

> What a wonderful change in my life has been wrought
> since Jesus came into my heart!
> I have light in my soul for which long I had sought,
> since Jesus came into my heart!

Deciding to live my life for Jesus was the best decision I have ever made. For, besides the joy and peace that I received, there was also a renewed sense that there was a plan for my life – and this was God's plan. A vital part of this plan began to unveil two years after my encounter with Jesus. While I was growing in my faith through prayer, Bible study and a commitment to opening my life to the guidance of the Holy Spirit at every turn, I started feeling a compelling sense to leave my successful job as a teacher of Maths and Physics for a full-time ministry. This came about as a real growing passion to share my faith and serve God's people began to develop in me, to the point that nothing else in my life satisfied me except this. After seeking God's will, I got a clear confirmation when my home church decided to send me to a theological institution to be better prepared for ministry.

Because of my desire to follow God's call, at various stages of my life, I have been called upon to risk everything and start all over again. I recall, for instance, my adventure of faith as my family and I left our native country for Kenya, in 2001, to pursue further studies that were to be done in English, a language which I was unable to speak or write at the time! Surprisingly however, this move turned out to be another step into the fulfilment of God's big plan for me. For it is there in Kenya that God opened unexpected doors to me through a lecturer, who, as a graduate of the University of Aberdeen, suggested that I come to Scotland (a country then unknown to me) for my doctoral studies. Now I am in Scotland, and the rest is, as they say, history!

STILL EXPLORING

Donald MacEwan

University Chaplain, University of St Andrews ■

This book is nearly over. Something led you to pick it up, and continue until now. I hope you have truly explored over its sections – explored your faith, God, Jesus and the Spirit, belonging to the Church, being committed to God's world and to his people. As in any true exploration, there will have been some confusing directions, wrong turnings and tedious stretches. Some of the food will have been stodgy, or unpalatable. It won't always have been a comfortable ride. And as with all exploring, the real change is in the one who explores. The territory becomes mapped, but the one who looks, who sees, who records and who describes is never the same again.

It is deeply satisfying to live as we are called to live.

I hope that you have found or will find faith, belief in God. It is deeply satisfying to live as we are called to live. And, if so, I hope you feel able to belong to the Church. Rumours of the Church's demise, in Scotland and beyond, are widespread and persistent. Yet you are a witness to a different rumour, of trust and love, of commitment and community, of hope in the face of suffering.

If you have read this on your own, I suggest you explore churches nearby you, and find one which is welcoming, understanding and full of integrity. It will probably be as flawed as it is friendly, but still the Spirit will be there. If you have read this with others, I hope that you now feel part of a community of explorers, who are mapping new territory together, and becoming friends.

What is next? There are as many *nexts* as there are readers. Living out the promises of baptism or confirmation is a lifetime's gift, a lifetime's task. God doesn't stop loving us, the world doesn't stop needing love, and there is never any reason to get bored. As soon as maps are published, they're out of date. We're always still exploring. ■

READ

John 15:1–17 Abide, love, bear fruit

THINK

1. How will you continue to explore?

2. Is there a church nearby that you might consider attending?

3. Where do you want to go from here?

ACT

Write down one thing that has changed in you since reading this book.